Leon Burton
Kathy Kuroda

ArtsPlay

Creative Activities
in Dance, Drama, Art, and Music
for Young Children

 Addison-Wesley Publishing Company
Menlo Park, California • Reading, Massachusetts
London • Amsterdam • Don Mills, Ontario • Sydney

Acknowledgement

Special thanks to California Young World, Mountain View, California, Terry Shue, Director, where the photographs in this book were taken.

Teachers: Kathleen Auby, Karen Elma, Lenore Nungester, B. Devin Wilson

Children: Jessica Adams, Jay Ambler, Stacy Blenio, Teresa Buckner, Shantel Byrd, Karina Cantre, Brandon Collins, Susan and Maili Cooper, Christian Delton, Vinh Phuc Doan, Shondra Dockter, Chris Dumont, Ava Fong, Edwin and Erick Fletcher, Latrina Fletcher, Natalie Fong, Brian Buzman, Jessica and Gwen Harry, Julie and Nikki Hudson, Jynette Hackett, Tracey Hayes, Preston Jackson, Butchie and Artie Jones, Joyce Jones, Kimberlee Lord, Shannon Mardirosian, David Moore, Tuong Nguyen, Sara O'Neal, Melissa del Pilar, Tiffany Roetkin, Dipali and Kartik Shah, Joshua Visher, Howard Wang.

Book Design: Wendy Palmer Associates, Palo Alto, California

Contents

Introduction

Young children are curious and filled with fantasy! As soon as
they learn to reach and crawl, they embark on explorations to all
accessible areas. They look, listen, grasp, taste, throw, push, hit,
pull, shake, bite—they attempt some kind of physical contact with
all objects that catch their attention. With gusto, they move onward
to explore new frontiers, ever searching for new objects, new
sounds, new experiences.

Natural curiosity and the desire to explore are qualities we prize
in young children—in children at all ages—for curiosity and an
inquiring mind are important components of creative thought and
action. The responsibility of all who educate is to promote the
further development of these characteristics in young children.

The intent of this book of activities is to foster young children's
natural creativity. The activities are based on the arts, as avenues of
self-expression through which individual creativity is stimulated.
They spark development of originality, imagination, independence,
spontaneity, openness, intuition, inquiry, and interest in investiga-
tion and exploration. Each person is endowed at birth with creative
potential; if not given an opportunity to flower, that potential will
lie dormant for a lifetime, all the time any of us have.

CONTENT AREAS IN THE ARTS

Each activity is organized around one or more content areas in
dance, drama, art, and music. This focuses the activities, providing
a base from which creative thought and action proceed.

The content areas selected are those most appropriate for young
children. Should you have had previous experience in one or more

of the arts, you may decide to organize additional creative activities for your children that embrace areas other than those:

Art	Dance	Music	Drama
line	movement	tone	pantomime
color	space	rhythm	dialog
shape	force	melody	improvisation
texture	time	harmony	role-playing
design		texture	dramatization
		form	
		tonality	

Prior to an activity, you and your children should have some familiarity with the content area(s) specified. You can conduct a brief preactivity to introduce the children to the activity's content area(s). Suggestions are included in the section **The Teacher's Homework**. Following are descriptions of the various content areas:

Art: Line, Color, Shape, Texture, Design

Line is the track made by a moving point; a line is therefore longer than it is wide.

Color is red, yellow, and blue, or some combination of the three.

Shape is an area of specific character defined by an outline, or by a contrasting color or texture of the surrounding area.

Texture is the "surface feel" of an object or the representation of surface character. Texture is the actual and "visual feel" of surface areas as they are altered by man and nature. Actual textures are material surfaces, which, when touched, stimulate characteristic sensory responses.

Design is the framework on which the artist bases the formal organization of his or her work. In a broader sense, it is synonymous with the term "form."

Dance: Movement, Space, Force, Time

Movement is the use of the body and its parts to communicate feelings, ideas, images, interpretations. Movement includes walking, running, leaping, jumping, hopping, skipping, galloping, sliding, shimmering, swinging, swaying, collapsing, twisting, bending, stretching, jerking, turning, spinning.

Space is the area occupied by the body, whether stationary or moving. The body can achieve a variety of geometric, abstract, and representational shapes at different *levels* (high, medium, low). Both moving and stationary body shapes range in *size* (wide, narrow, large, small), and all moving body shapes have *direction* (forward, sideward, backward, circular).

Force is the manner in which energy is used in movement. Movements may be *strong, light, smooth, percussive*.

Time is the period of time, or interval, during which movements are executed. Most movements have an underlying *beat*—the speed of these beats is *tempo*. *Accents* are certain beats within a metric unit that are emphasized. Repeated patterns of long and short movements in time establish *rhythm patterns*.

Music: Tone, Rhythm, Melody, Harmony, Texture, Form, Tonality

Tone, or sound, has four basic characteristics. The characteristics higher and lower are called *pitch*. *Duration* is the longer and shorter characteristics of sound. *Loudness* is the relative degree of loudness and softness. *Timbre* is the quality of sound that helps us differentiate between wood, metal, human voices, musical instruments, and other sources of sound.

Rhythm is one of the most magnetic aspects of music. The pulsating characteristic of music is called *beat*. *Tempo* is the rate of speed (faster and slower) of beats. *Accelerando* describes beats that gradually increase in speed or tempo; *Ritardando* describes beats that gradually slow down. The succession of longer and shorter durations that establishes patterns of sound is called *rhythm pattern*.

Melody is the linear succession of sounds of different pitches and durations. The upward and downward movement of pitches gives a general shape to music—*contour*. Sounds in a melody performed in a smooth, connected way are *legato*. Sounds performed in a separated, detached manner are *staccato*.

Harmony is the musical effect of different pitches sounding at the same time. A *chord* is the sounding together of three or more different pitches.

Texture is the musical effect of one or more different parts sounding together. *Accompaniment* is the supportive role to a melody or to another part intended to be in the foreground.

Form describes how *sections* or other units of musical selections combine to create a whole. *Repetition* refers to sections within a musical selection that are repeated. Sections different from each other are referred to as *contrast*.

Tonality is the tonal center or gravitational pull of one pitch in a melody or other musical selection. This tonal center is called the *tonic* or "home tone."

Drama: Pantomine, Dialog, Improvisation, Role-Playing, Dramatization

Pantomime is drama presented by mimics using bodily movement without the aid of speech or song, sometimes accompanied by instrumental music.

Dialog is the conversational element of dramatic action, the words people use in communication. It is verbalization growing out of the life of a scene or event.

Improvisation is acting, singing, composing, or reciting on the spur of the moment. There is no story line or plot, and the problem is solved by spontaneously making up a part (playing it by ear).

Role-playing is the process of becoming a character (person, animal, inanimate object), either assigned or assumed. It is putting oneself into the position of another, assuming those characteristics.

Dramatization is the sum total of all dramatic action (events, scenes, dialog, acting, role-playing, characterization, improvisation, pantomime, etc.).

THE NATURE OF CREATIVITY

What is creativity? What are the characteristics of creative persons? Why is it important that young children develop their creative potentials? Should specially planned environments be provided for young children to encourage original thinking and stimulate creative action? In what ways will the development of creative thinking enrich their lives in later years? These are questions that should be seriously considered by all involved with instruction for young children, whether in the home, church, private preschool, public early childhood centers, or schools. Creative imagination peaks in young children around age four to four and one-half, then begins to decline about age five as a result of cultural, social, and other influences. An important goal in early childhood education, therefore, is to stimualte young children's creative imagination and encourage its continuing development.

What is Creativity?

Creativity is a process of combining known factors (knowledge, skills) into new relationships to produce new results—a new product, a new way of thinking and perceiving, a new way of performing.

Creativity is not some kind of magical process that defies understanding. It is not an inherited quality a child has from highly creative parents, and it should not be confused with talent and general intelligence. Creativity is a process of inventing, experimenting with new and previously learned information and skills in new and interesting ways. Creativity is stepping into the unknown, getting off the main track, breaking out of a mold, being open to new experiences, permitting ideas to be recombined and letting one thing lead to another, and building new relationships among ideas. It is freeing one's self from established routines of perception and action, redefining situations, acting in new roles called for by the situation. Although often approached by group activity in educational settings, creativity is an individual—not a group—experience.

What Are the Characteristics of Creative Persons?

interest in ideas and meanings
eagerness to explore the environment because of a need to know
willingness to risk the unknown
openness to new experiences, ideas
high tolerance of ambiguity
interest in personal expression
preference for complexity

persistence in examining
sensitivity to problems
spontaneity
curiosity
originality
imagination
courage
playfulness
flexibility
independence
intuitiveness

Highly creative persons are never simpletons—they are fairly intelligent but few have phenomenal IQs. Beyond a certain point, increased intelligence does not determine the level of a person's creative ability.

People create for different reasons: as an expression of the self for personal fulfillment, to meet external needs and goals, as an expression of the self while solving an external problem.

There are two types of creative persons. One type is generally healthy, alert, lives in the real world, perceptive, humorous, spontaneous, expressive, daring, and has a natural sense of curiosity. The other type is less at ease with himself and the world. He or she prefers mental operations to working with people, likes working in isolation, and has a high degree of control over personal impulses. Both types of creative persons seem to have a

preference for asymmetry
passion for synthesizing
independence in relation to others
tolerance for ambiguity, disorder, tension, conflict
ability to hold personal views regardless of pressure

Creative persons are often described as nonconformists. The nonconformity, however, may lie only in the realm of ideas, not necessarily in behavior. A creative person may conform consistently to social rules of conduct, while using his or her energies to follow personal interests and setting goals that conflict with the goals of others.

Why is it Important That Young Children Develop Their Creative Potentials?

A direct relationship exists between the development of a person's creative ability and the likelihood he or she will become a fully functioning, mentally healthy, well-educated, and vocationally successful individual. Children from a very early age are confronted with problems to solve. Problem solving requires thinking, and a child whose creative potential has been neglected will take only a conventional approach to a solution. The child approaches a problem depending on facts already known; the ability to think is limited to existing knowledge and methods. He or she therefore has limited ability to cope with challenging situations. This is called "convergent thinking."

The creative child will approach problem solving by looking for links between past experience and something not previously considered. This child's thinking may go in several directions at once, producing a range of possible solutions. He or she unhesitatingly reaches into the unknown and is flexible and original in finding solutions. This is called "divergent thinking."

Both kinds of thinking are important and of great value in the young child's world. But a creative environment is essential to the development of divergent thinking. Young children who develop both kinds of thinking expand their world view, find the challenge of problem solving less threatening, and are better able to cope with life's increasingly complex situations as they grow.

Should Specially Planned Environments Be Provided for Young Children to Encourage Original Thinking and Stimulate Creative Action?

The educational environment of young children is all-important to the development of creative thinking. As mentioned earlier, creative imagination begins to decline about age five. Much of this decline may be prevented by giving young children learning and play environments that encourage rather than stifle creative thought.

Some environments promote creativity; others discourage it. Young children subjected primarily to rote and recall activities—rather than decision-making and problem-solving activities—will be limited in their creative development. Environments that cause anxiety in children also stifle creativity. When all learning and play experiences are strictly controlled, there will be little creative thought. Here are other features of educational settings that block the development of creative thought:

> giving in to social pressure by constantly reminding children to be realistic and stop imagining
>
> approving only those behaviors that follow established traditions
>
> establishing conditions that cause children to be fearful of taking a new approach
>
> strict control that limits or prohibits questioning and exploration
>
> placing too high a value on conformity in all activities
>
> holding children back, waiting for their readiness
>
> an overemphasis on memorization
>
> too many rigid, routinely organized tasks

Some people believe that all group processes inhibit creative thinking. This suggests a great need for activities in which children work alone, and others in which they work toward individual expression within a group context.

Environments that stimulate creativity give children opportunities to:

> contribute original ideas
>
> share differing points of view
>
> seek new ways to look at problems
>
> keep their fantasies alive
>
> develop research and inquiry skills

Informality is an important feature of the creative environment. Young children need to feel free to participate in activities and even exchange roles on occasion. A feeling of trust and equality among all children in the group and the teacher is essential. Such an educational climate requires a skilled teacher who is not domineering.

Another interesting feature of this environment is having situations that cause children moderate stress. Too little stress will result in children failing to focus the problem, and too much stress will generate rigidity. Young children need enough uncertainty and stress to stimulate innovation, along with enough security to offset the anxiety that uncertainty brings.

In What Ways Will the Development of Creative Potential Enrich the Lives of Young Children in Later Years?

A high level of creative ability is not essential or appropriate to certain occupations. But the development of creative potential does contribute significantly to people's functioning, so they make better life choices. Reasoning powers are heightened—they look and really see, listen and really hear. The level of awareness is increased, bringing greater sensitivity to situations in life.

Those who develop their creative potentials are less anxious and have fewer authoritarian attitudes. Less creative persons are typically oriented toward quick achievement; they want to impose order immediately, to synthesize things early. More creative persons work slowly at first, then move quickly to synthesis. Creative persons generally have more self-confidence and wide-ranging interests. They know when to be disciplined, when to exercise rigor. Rigor and discipline are essential—the more comfortable people are, the less creative they are likely to be.

Creative persons cultivate more independent personal tastes than do the less creative. The creative generate new knowledge, they conceptualize ways of imposing higher levels of order, thus making more significant contributions in all areas of life. The less creative are usually bound to what is, the more creative to what could be. *The greater young children's creative potential is developed, the more enriched their lives can become.*

THE ACTIVITIES

This book has 100 creative activities. Some are designed for individual experience, others for group experience. Many of the group activities may be adapted for individuals, and some of the individual activities may be used for the group. All activities are listed in the **Table of Contents** by title and page number.

Format of the Activities

A single format is used for all 100 activities. Each has a title that relates to one or more of the arts and, in some instances, to a product resulting from creative experience. The arts content areas of the activities appear above the titles. Suggestions for brief, preliminary activities in those areas are included in the section **The Teacher's Homework**.

Next is a description of the activity's product, with an indication of the kind of creative operation involved. Pictures of children in action show important features of the activities. Some pictures will show items you need to make prior to beginning.

The **Activity** section summarizes the procedures and describes the product children will create.

The main section of the activity is titled **Procedure**. This is a step-by-step procedure for beginning the activity and guiding it to completion. You may elect to personalize the procedures after becoming familiar with the activity plan. Many activities may be adapted to accommodate your children's and your own interests and abilities. The procedures do not provide a complete dialog appropriate for all children in all situations. Therefore, in some activities you must improvise a dialog (side coaching) to stimulate creative thought and action. In an improvised dialog, you question and comment to help children when they encounter roadblocks. The dialog will help them use their creative imaginations to solve problems.

The purpose of the procedures is to guide the development of creative potential. Therefore, accuracy, highly refined products, and polished performances are not primary goals. The procedures suggest ways to stimulate creative development and work toward refinement while having an enjoyable, learning, and play experience. We urge you to keep this purpose in mind should you decide to adjust the procedures.

Supplementary Activity is the next section, which guides children in follow-up creative activities that utilize the skills and understandings they developed earlier. The purpose here is reinforcement.

The last section, **Materials**, lists all items needed to conduct the activities. Art supplies, props, instructions for making props, sound sources, musical instruments, equipment, recordings, assorted objects, furniture, etc., are listed. The items for the supplementary activity are those marked with an asterisk.

Individual Activities

Most of the individual activities are in art and music, and may be used in any sequence. You can adapt some of the group activities for individual experience. Before starting the individual activities, you should explain to the children that materials may be checked out from you as time is made available for individual work. Stimulate their curiosity by showing some containers of materials for the activities. Children will especially be interested in materials stored in attractive boxes, and in activities that require unusual props and equipment.

Choose one or two individual activities to demonstrate procedures to the children. Explain this three-step plan.

1. At the beginning, you will work with the child for a short period. Here, you will give directions, demonstrate equipment, designate a place to work, and help the child get underway.
2. Next, leave the child to work alone. If necessary, he or she requests help from you or another child who has completed the activity. Some activities take only a few minutes; others take longer.
3. Finally, the child shows you, or asks you to listen to, the creation. You might discuss this, encouraging the child and stimulating interest in other creative activities.

If you keep a cumulative folder for each child, be certain to record completion of the activity. You might comment on how well the child was able to follow the procedures and his or her general interest in the creation.

Group Activities

Most of the book's activities are designed for group experience. They may be used in any sequence, but it is highly recommended that *Balloon Persons, Frog Jumps, Popcorn, Falling Leaves, Sea Anemone, Let's Go Skating,* and *Ice Creatures* be completed before you introduce the other dance activities. These seven will help the children build certain skills and understandings that will contribute to their success in the other dance activities.

The section **The Nature of Creativity** stated that although creativity is often approached as a group activity in educational settings, it is an individual—not a group—experience. It is important that, in the group activities, you encourage personal expression and uniqueness. The child's creative experience will result from participation in the activity. You might approach the group activities as a collection of individual creations that together produce interesting creative results.

Level of Difficulty of Activities

Some activities are more difficult than others. A wide range has been included to accommodate the needs and interests of
(1) children who are older or are progressing faster than others,

and (2) children who are younger or need repeated experiences and reinforcement.

Several activities are designed for older and more experienced children. However, in some instances, parts of these could be completed by younger or less-experienced children. Following are suggestions for adapting parts of activities you believe are too difficult for the children in your group.

Body Part Designs (p. 188): Younger or less-experienced children may have difficulty moving their body parts creatively to draw a variety of shapes. Their objective, then, can be to become familiar with only one shape, using only one or two body parts to draw it in the air. Should they participate in the Supplementary Activity, they can simply move their body parts (on your cue) in time with the music, making no effort to draw a shape.

Ice Cream Shop (p. 42): Younger children may not be familiar with the physical features of an ice cream shop, and thus could not role-play an ice cream shop scene and improvise appropriate dialog. You could adapt the activity by naming a few physical features of an ice cream shop and deciding on an imaginary layout for the children. You could then improvise a dialog and have the children pantomine it.

Drum Improvisation (p. 140): This activity requires the child to use two drums of different pitch and include examples of loud and soft in his improvisation. A younger child will probably be more successful using only one drum to improvise rhythms in time with the recorded music. Eliminate the requirement of loud and soft to reduce the variables for the child.

Spray Painting (p. 112): A less-experienced child may have difficulty operating the spray attachment and arranging the positive and negative cutouts. The activity could be adapted by having an older child operate the sprays and assist as requested by the less-experienced child.

For how many activities must you prepare materials to get underway? It depends on how quickly you want to use the activities. Some teachers prepare materials for only one or two activities at a time; others prepare for many so they will have a wider selection to accommodate the children's varied interests. Whichever approach you use, prepare materials to withstand repeated use. Adequate storage areas and a simple identification and location system for materials will be needed.

Masters for several activities are included in the Appendix. It is intended that these be used *ONLY* if you feel your children need this kind of help. If your children are able to create bird, tree, and face drawings without the masters, their creative experience will be heightened.

THE TEACHER'S HOMEWORK

It is important that you read the introductory material carefully before beginning the activities. Scan the **Contents** page, familiarize yourself with the activities and their format, become acquainted with the appendices. You might then study many activities before selecting those for the children's earliest experiences.

Before getting the activities underway, be certain that you have prepared yourself adequately in the identified arts content areas. It also is recommended that you plan and present to the children brief preactivity experiences. This will ensure that they have some understanding of the content areas in which they will focus their creative experience. Children with previous experience will be reinforced in the content areas. Also, this will permit you to introduce the content areas to children who might have recently joined your group.

Some content areas are more easily understood than others. You will need to decide which areas need additional attention, how much time and explanation you should invest. Here are several examples of preactivity experiences for your children:

Art: Line	Have the children draw long, short, straight, curved, crooked, jagged lines on paper using pencils, crayons, felt-tip pens.
Art: Design	Have the children help you arrange blocks and/or tinker toys into various designs (a park, a playground, a house, a store, etc.).
Dance: Space	Use a bookshelf and have the children place books on shelves at different levels (high, medium, low). Then have them walk with two fingers in different directions (forward, sideward, backward, circular). To illustrate size, draw for them clown faces that are wide, narrow, large, small.
Dance: Force	Ask the children to march with strong steps, then with light steps. Have them move their arms in the air smoothly as clouds would move, then make motions as if they are holding a hammer and pounding big nails.
Music: Rhythm	Have the children walk in a circle to the beat as you play a drum. Play slow

	beats, fast beats, beats that gradually become faster (accelerando), beats that gradually slow down (ritardando). Play a repeated rhythm pattern such as long-short-short, long-short-short, long-short-short, and have them move to it.
Music: Texture	Have the children sing a familiar song with you. Repeat, having them accompany by clapping their hands to the beat. For a third singing they could tap their feet for an accompaniment.
Drama: Role-Playing	Ask the children to become (move and make sounds) the animals you name, such as dog, cat, tiger, bird, fish.
Drama: Pantomime	Have the children use movement (no sound) and act as if they are doing the activities you name, such as swimming, climbing a tree, flying through the air, taking a bath, dressing to go to school.

USE OF THIS BOOK WITH OTHER CURRICULUM MATERIALS IN THE ARTS

This book may be used by itself for the development of creative potential in the arts. But the activities can be used in conjunction with other curriculum materials (such as *MusicPlay: Learning Activities for Young Children*, Burton and Hughes, Addison-Wesley Publishing Company) and with activities you and others have designed. You may want to review all materials and teacher-designed activities you currently use, then decide how this book's activities could best be woven into your teaching plans. The format of the activities and the identification of arts content areas may give you ideas for designing other creative activities that relate directly to whatever materials and procedures you are presently using.

This book approaches creativity with the idea that understanding of arts content areas is essential. It suggests that learning new information and skills helps to stimulate creative activity. We highly recommend that you view *teaching* as an essential part of the total process. *Children cannot create unless they have the wherewithal with which to create.* We encourage you to help children acquire the "wherewithal" as needed, and to approach the activities as both learning and creative experiences for children.

SHARING THE RESULTS OF CREATIVE ACTIVITY

Evening meetings of parents, teachers, and children are excellent opportunities for you and your children to share results of some of the creative activities. You can have exhibits in school, children can take art work home to parents and friends. But sharing their creations in music, drama, and dance is more difficult. We recommend that you prepare some of the group activities to present to parents and others. Remember, highly polished presentations are not the objective. The objective is to demonstrate techniques that stimulate creative thought and action while encouraging self-expression through the arts.

RECORDING USED IN THIS BOOK

The recording that accompanies this book is essential to many of the activities. Each selection included in the record has been especially prepared for certain activities. It will be difficult, if not impossible, for you to find other recorded selections that will be appropriate substitutes.

Dance Activities

We recommend that you complete *Balloon Persons, Frog Jumps, Popcorn, Falling Leaves, Sea Anemone, Let's Go Skating,* and *Ice Creatures* prior to presenting other dance activities.

Balloon Persons

The children move creatively to role-play a balloon.

Activity

The children stretch, bend, twist, and collapse as they create a human balloon.

Procedure

Blow up a balloon and let the children observe the process. Then release it and let it fly and sputter around the room. Blow up the balloon again, this time tie a knot at the opening. Show the children how light the balloon is by tossing it in the air. Have them lightly tap it to each other to feel its weight. When you think the children understand the different characteristics of the balloon, ask them to imagine that they are human balloons that have an opening at the right big toe.

The children space themselves on the floor and make their bodies as small as they can (any position is acceptable). You begin "blowing up" the human balloons by making a blowing sound. You might have the human balloons partially fill with air, then suddenly collapse, requiring you to start the blowing sound again. Turn the balloons loose at any time and let them go flying and sputtering about the room. When all the human balloons are finally filled with air, tell them you are tying a knot at the right big toe opening. Then "narrate" the balloons through being blown gently by the wind and finally popping (when you touch their heads) with a loud sound.

Supplementary Activity

Blow up the human balloons again and take them on an adventure. For example, the balloons pass through a tornado (spinning and turning), get caught in a tree (twisting and turning), bounce along a sidewalk (jumping and hopping), get squeezed by some children (crunching up their bodies), slowly deflate (collapsing).

Materials

A balloon

Frog Jumps

The children move creatively to role-play a frog's activities.

Activity

The children jump and twist in creative ways to role-play a frog jumping about in search of food.

Procedure

Make ten circles (approximately 12″ in diameter) with masking tape on the floor, one to two feet apart. Briefly discuss with the children what a person does with his or her feet when jumping, then ask some to demonstrate. Help them recognize the difference between jumping and hopping (both feet leave the floor when jumping). Have groups of three or four take turns jumping from one circle to another.

Guide the children to explore twisting various parts of their bodies: head, torso, legs, arms, fingers, feet, etc. Have them twist in standing, kneeling, and lying positions.

Now ask them to sit in a circle around the ten circles on the floor. Explain that they are going to imagine they are frogs jumping from lily pad to lily pad in search of something to eat. You will signal when and how they should move. Sometimes they will jump, other times, twist. When they imagine a juicy mosquito flying by, they will twist to catch it in their mouths. Have the children, in groups of three or four, assume the frog role. Call out "jump, jump, jump, twist" (briefly pausing between signals for movement time). Use different signal combinations. They should try to be unique and creative in their frog roles, particularly in the way they twist and catch mosquitos.

*Supplementary Activity

Play the recording "Frog Music" and ask the children to listen for the music suggestion to jump and twist. The pattern of sounds in the recording is "jump, jump, jump, twist." When they recognize these features, ask them (in groups of three or four) to assume frog roles and move in response to the music. Stress the idea of making unique movements in time with the sounds in the music.

Materials

Masking tape

*Phonograph
Recording of "Frog Music"

Popcorn

The children move creatively as popcorn kernels.

Activity

The children move creatively as popcorn kernels in a pot that pop and achieve interesting shapes.

Procedure

Either clap your hands or tap a drum to a steady beat as children hop about the room in time with the beats. Help them distinguish between a hop and a jump (in a hop, one foot is always on the ground; in a jump, both feet leave the ground). Experiment with slowing down and speeding up. Help the children distinguish between the two. After exploring changes in speed, again clap or tap a steady beat. This time, play an occasional loud beat to signal that the children are to freeze in an interesting shape.

Next have the children sit in a circle. Every other child goes inside while the others stay in the circular pattern. The children in the circle are to imagine they are popcorn kernels inside a large pot. Pantomime pouring oil into the pot (circle) then turning on the stove. Tell the kernels of corn (children in the circle) that the stove is becoming hotter and hotter. The kernels should gradually begin to shake and squirm in the oil. As their movements become more intense and the pot is extremely hot, they begin to pop—freezing in an interesting shape just like popped corn. End the popping process by pouring carmel in the pot, causing all the popped kernels to stick together. The children in the circle then exchange places with those sitting and the process is repeated. Throughout the activity focus their attention on some of the more interesting shapes the children achieve.

*Supplementary Activity

Play the recording "Popcorn Music" and ask the children to listen for music that suggests kernels of corn popping. Ask all the children to imagine that the room is a big pot. Pantomime the process in the activity above, then start the music. The music repeats the heating and popping process several times. Encourage the children to make their popped shapes as unique as they can.

Materials

Drum with beater (optional)

*Phonograph
 Recording of "Popcorn Music"

Falling Leaves

The children move creatively to role-play falling leaves.

Activity

The children swing, sway, and turn their bodies to create a falling-leaves role.

Procedure

Ask the children to stand in one position and rock from side to side. Then they sway isolated body parts such as head, torso, arms. Eventually they stand in one position and sway their entire bodies with large movements. Have them experiment with turning movements.

Introduce the idea of swinging with a ball attached to a string. Demonstrate how a swing may move circularly or arch-like. Help them use energy in swinging movements with the arms: extend them up to the right, then drop them, swinging up to the left. Have them swing isolated parts of their bodies (head, torso, arms, hands), and eventually their entire bodies.

Ask the children to imagine that they are leaves on a tree (you may role-play a tree), ready to fall off because winter is coming. When you call out "autumn leaves are falling" they are to begin swinging and swaying their bodies. Finally, the leaves (children) break off from the branches and in swinging, swaying, turning movements gradually fall to the ground. When the leaves land on the ground, they are to freeze in interesting shapes. Coach the children as they need help; particularly focus attention on children who have created interesting movements and shapes. Help them explore many different ways to turn, sway, and swing their bodies.

Repeat the process several times, then have the children divide into groups. The groups will take turns performing and watching.

*Supplementary Activity

Have the children repeat the activity in response to the recording "Falling Leaves Music." They can use scarves to represent the blowing wind moving the falling leaves.

Materials

Ball with string attached (optional)

*Phonograph
 Recording of "Falling Leaves Music"
 Scarves (lightweight material)

Sea Anemone

The children extend and contract their bodies in creative ways.

Activity

The children move their bodies creatively and achieve a variety of extended and contracted positions at three different levels.

Procedure

Ask the children to stand and stretch their bodies into interesting shapes. Explain that you will clap your hands while they are stretching—they should freeze on the fourth clap. Next time, the children contract their bodies to make them as small as possible, again freezing in an interesting position on the fourth clap. Have the children repeat this procedure kneeling, then lying down. Pause during the activity for children to share some of the extended and contracted shapes they achieve at the three different levels.

*Supplementary Activity

Either show the children a picture of a sea anemone or arrange to have a worm ball in the classroom. Explain how this kind of water creature may extend or stretch its body and tentacles, then contract when in danger. Tell the children they will now become this kind of water creature. Divide them into three small groups and position the groups near each other. Within each group some should stand, some should kneel, and some should lie flat. Explain that you are going to tell a story, and that they—as water creatures—will perform the actions suggested.

"In the deep, blue sea lived three sea anemones that swayed their long tentacles with the current of the ocean. Their long arms reached out and caught tiny animals swimming by. The anemones pulled the animals in and fed themselves (at this point focus their attention on some of the interesting ways children are stretching their arms and legs). The three anemones were busy catching food one day when, suddenly, a big fish swam by. The anemones quickly pulled back their long tentacles and made themselves as small as they could. When the big fish swam away, they slowly began to stretch out their bodies and tentacles."

Repeat the story several times to let all children move at the three different levels. You may want to select recorded music for background as you tell the story.

Materials

*Pictures of a sea anemone, or a worm ball (Tubifex worm) which may be purchased from a pet store

Let's Go Skating

The children move creatively while wearing imaginary skates.

Activity

The children move creatively in different directions while skating on imaginary skates.

Procedure

Demonstrate for the children how to move forward, backward, and sideward by sliding your feet on the floor. Then have the children slide and move in different directions, experimenting with fast and slow slides. After a period of exploration, invite the children to move and imagine they are skating. They may wear imaginary roller or ice skates. Suggest they add some tricks to their skating such as turning, skating backward, doing hops and leaps, walking on the toes of the skates.

Ask the children to sit in a circle. Explain how you wish them to move during their next skating activity. As you clap your hands, you also will call out specific skating instructions. For example, you may say "slide, slide, slide, slide, turn, freeze." After they freeze into an interesting shape, call out another set of instructions such as "slide, turn, slide, leap, turn, freeze." Continue, naming other patterns of specific movement. Eventually select some children to demonstrate their movements for others.

Now have the children make up their own combinations of skating movements. Clap your hands six times; they make any movement they wish on the five claps, but they freeze in position on the sixth.

*Supplementary Activity

Invite the children to "go skating" with you as they listen to "Skater's Waltz." Ask them to skate in whatever direction they wish, but to include turns, leaps, hops, and to move in time with the music.

Materials

*Phonograph
Recording of "Skater's Waltz"

Ice Creatures

The children move creatively and freeze in response to drum sounds.

Activity

The children move creatively in response to drum beats, and freeze in interesting shapes when they hear a loud beat.

Procedure

Discuss with the children the difference between moving and being in a stationary position. You could illustrate the idea by swinging your arms until a child says "freeze." Invite the children to stand and move in response to the beats as you play the drum. Suggest they do a variety of movements such as walk, skip, slide, sway, and continue to move until you say "freeze." They then achieve an interesting pose, as if frozen in position.

Now ask the children to imagine they are magical creatures who freeze in interesting shapes every time they hear a loud sound. Play drum beats as a signal for them to begin moving. When you play a loud, accented beat, they become frozen ice creatures and do not move until the drum beats begin again. Side coach the children to encourage originality as they create frozen shapes.

Supplementary Activity

Have the children in groups of three create ice sculptures with each child in a different level. As you play fast beats on the drum, a child begins running, then freezes at one level on a loud beat. The first child holds his position, and the second begins running as the drum beats start again; on the loud beat the second connects to the frozen first child at a different level. Continue the procedure until the three children are connected, frozen into an interesting sculpture at three different levels. Finally, signal the children to melt. Repeat the process for the next three children. Encourage the children to connect themselves in original ways to create a sculpture.

Materials

Drum with beater

Shadow Creatures

The children use their bodies to create a variety of shadow creatures.

Activity

The children use their bodies to create a variety of shadow creatures, which are projected onto a sheet screen.

Procedure

Have the children take turns creating a shadow creature. Explain that you will tap a drum softly for nine counts, and that a child behind a sheet screen should move until the loud beat of count ten. Then the child freezes in position for a few seconds so those watching may enjoy the creature created. The child must freeze close to the sheet so his or her creature is visible. After each child has had a turn, have pairs create interesting shapes together. You may eventually elect to have a small group create creatures. Guide the children to discover different ways to create body shapes singly, in pairs, and in small groups.

*Supplementary Activity

Give the children assorted cellophane cutouts with which to create creatures, using their bodies in combination with the cutouts. Selected objects may eventually be included to create even more interesting shadow creatures.

Materials

Large white or pastel-colored sheet to use as a projection screen (hang the sheet on a line or wooden frame with space in front for an audience and space in back for a projector and a small group of children)

Line, rope, or wooden frame

Slide projector or another source of light (placed behind the sheet, leaving sufficient space for children to move between the projector and the sheet)

Weights to keep the sheet stationary

Drum with beater

*Assorted colored cellophane cutouts with cardboard frames such as the following:

Bubble Popping

The children move creatively to pop bubbles.

Activity

The children use their bodies and body parts in creative ways to pop bubbles.

Procedure

Use chalk (or some other material) to draw six circles approximately 18″ in diameter on the floor. Have children stand in the circles. Use the bubblemaker to make bubbles; scatter them so they will float within the children's circles. As the bubbles float within their range, the children remain in their circles and "pop" them with different body parts (elbow, head, shoulder, bottom, knee, foot, nose, finger, etc.). After a brief period of popping, begin again. This time they modify their movements to be as artistic as possible. For instance, before popping a bubble, they twist, spin, jump, shake, use slow motion, extend the body. Children could perform individually, sharing their more refined "popping" movements. Eventually invite another six children to have a turn in the circles.

*Supplementary Activity

Play the recording "Bubble Popping Music" and ask the children where the music cues them to pop bubbles. They will notice immediately the loud accents on the first of each four beats. Play the recording as you make bubbles and they stand in their circles. They are to pop bubbles *only* on the loud, accented beats. As always, they are to make their movements as original as possible.

Materials

Bottle of liquid bubbles with bubblemaker

*Phonograph
 Recording of "Bubble Popping Music"

Cocoon Shapes

The children create a variety of shapes with their bodies.

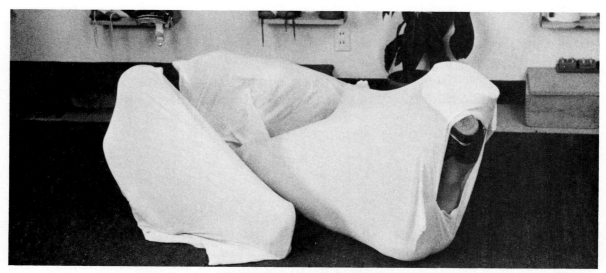

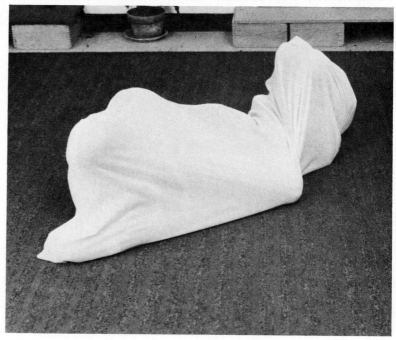

Activity

The children enter bags and create a variety of shapes by moving their bodies in different ways.

Procedure

Show the pictures of cocoons to the children and describe how certain insects are hatched from cocoons—how the baby insects twist, squirm, and move to free themselves from the cocoon. Then invite three children to go inside the "cocoon bags." Ask them to imagine they are baby insects twisting, turning, trying to get out. They should experiment moving, trying to make their bodies into many different shapes. When the children have explored their space within the bags, ask them to move while you tap a drum or clap your hands for ten counts. They freeze in position on the tenth count. Help the children watching to notice the variety of shapes created. All the children in the group take a turn creating shapes in the bags. If some are afraid to go into a bag alone, you may want to use one larger bag in which three children could share the space, as pictured on the previous page.

*Supplementary Activity

Play the recording "Waltz-Tremolo," to which three children at a time move in the cocoon bags. Encourage them to move as creatively as possible to the two contrasting sections of music.

Materials

Three bags made of stretchable,
   polyester, porous material
   as illustrated
Pictures of insect cocoons
Drum with beater (optional)
One bag 3′ x 5′ (optional)

*Phonograph
  Recording of "Waltz-Tremolo"

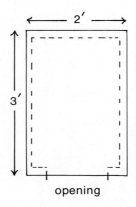

opening

Ribbon Dance

The children use ribbon props to create a dance.

Activity

The children use their bodies and ribbon props to create a dance in response to recorded music.

Procedure

Demonstrate for the children how to use their bodies and one of the ribbon props to create interesting movements and lines. Eventually invite children in groups of six to experiment with the ribbon props. Space them so their ribbons will not become tangled. Encourage originality as you side coach the children—suggest they try out slow, fast, large, small, smooth, jagged movements.

Play the recording "Ribbon Dance," to which the children create a dance with their ribbon props. Suggest they explore different levels, sizes, directions, and movements (leaps, hops, slides, etc.) as they move creatively to the music. Encourage them to do something different each time the tempo changes.

Supplementary Activity

To extend this activity play the recording again and have some children, without ribbon props, create a dance by moving in and out of ribbon lines created by those with props. A game of follow-the-leader can be played; the leader (without a prop) originates a movement that the others imitate. A new leader is named each time the tempo changes.

Materials

Four to six ribbon props: a piece of ribbon 6' long and 1" wide, connected with masking tape to a 9" dowel stick (½" in diameter)
Phonograph
Recording of "Ribbon Dance"

Through the Hula Hoops

The children move creatively through hula hoops.

Activity

The children move creatively through a series of hula hoops held in different positions.

Procedure

Have children hold the hula hoops in different positions. Other children follow as you go through the hoops doing a variety of movements. Then play the recording "Movement Music," to which the children go one-by-one through each of the hoops in an interesting way. This time they must use their imaginations. They may use movements such as wiggling, dancing, tumbling, slow motion, mechanical toy, slithering, shaking, swimming, hopping, crawling. Eventually invite those holding the hoops to have a turn.

Supplementary Activity

Invite the children to think of new ways to position the hoops. Have them take turns being leader—the other children have to imitate the leader's movements. Play the recording again as they move.

Materials

Three to six hula hoops
Phonograph
Recording of "Movement Music"

Smooth and Shaky

The children move creatively in response to sounds in a recording.

Activity

The children create unique movements to represent contrasting sounds they hear in a recording.

Procedure

Play the recording "Waltz-Tremolo" and invite the children to move freely to what they hear. Guide them to discover the contrasting sections in the music: one section with an obvious beat of 1-2-3, 1-2-3, 1-2-3; the other with fast, tremolo sounds having no recognizable beat. Also help them discover through movement the changes in tempo and levels of loudness, and the sudden absences of sound between sections. After one or two periods of listening and moving, ask the children to move again as they listen, striving for original movements. Have children who make interesting movements perform individually for different sections.

*Supplementary Activity

Give the children assorted rhythm instruments. They take turns improvising sounds in response to the contrasting sections of the recording.

Materials

Phonograph
Recording of "Waltz-Tremolo"

*Assorted rhythm instruments (one for each child)

Sheet and Body Sculptures

The children create interesting shapes using their bodies and a large sheet.

Activity

In small groups, the children take turns creating interesting shapes by going underneath a sheet and moving until they hear a signal to suspend movement and freeze in position.

Procedure

Ask four to six children to join you underneath the sheet as the others watch. Tell the children under the sheet to move—pull, twist, wrap, stretch—with you until you signal them to freeze like statues. After several seconds of moving, say "freeze." Those children watching can enjoy the shapes created by the bodies and the sheet. Repeat several times.

Have other groups take turns under the sheet without you. You may want to signal the children to freeze by using a drum. Softly tap the drum for nine counts; hit the drum hard on count ten which the children will learn to recognize as the freeze signal. When they hear the soft taps again, they move until the loud beat, and so on. Encourage them to achieve a variety of poses such as standing, kneeling, curling, sitting, lying flat with and without limbs extended. One child could hold onto an edge of the sheet to create puffs and add more variety to the shapes.

*Supplementary Activity

Play the recording "Floating Music" and invite a group of children to create shapes underneath the sheet. The music suggests moments to freeze in position. You may want to project a strong beam of light underneath the sheet to create shadows, adding another visual dimension to the sheet sculptures. You also could project the film from the *Film Making* activity onto the sheet for interesting results.

Materials

Large sheet
Drum with beater

*Phonograph
 Recording of "Floating Music"
 Light for projection
 Film

Spider's Dance

The children create a spider role.

Activity

The children use cord fastened to objects to build a spider's web; they then move through the web in interesting ways to create a spider's dance.

Procedure

The children stretch and bend with you, achieving interesting shapes with their bodies. After a few minutes of exploration through movement, discuss with the children how spiders spin their webs. Tell how the spider connects its web to objects as protection against the wind, and how it builds its web as a kind of net to catch prey.

Have the children play-act spiders who begin spinning a web. They move as spiders do, connect silken web thread to one object, move across to another object, etc. Eventually have them help you create a web using the rope or cord. Connect one end of the cord to an object, move as a spider does across to another object, connect it there. Pass the cord to a child, who spins the next part of the web. The first child passes the cord to the second, and so on. The object is to create a web of lines running all over the area you are using. Encourage originality as the children spin the web.

When the web is completed, play the recording "Spider's Dance" and begin to move through the web as a spider. The spider should reach, stretch, turn, bend, and swing as it moves from one thread to another. The children do their spider's dance in groups of three. As the music continues, encourage them to move through the web in interesting ways, trying different body shapes.

Supplementary Activity

You may extend the activity by creating a short story about some bugs that get caught in a web, and the spider wrapping them in silken thread. Have the children help you create the story, then play-act the different events. The recording "Spider's Dance" is good background music for the story.

Materials

Space in a room or on the playground that has stationary objects (jungle gym, table legs, etc.)
50' to 100' of rope or heavy cord wound on a stick
Phonograph
Recording of "Spider's Dance"

Body and String Shapes

The children create shapes and explore the concept of space through use of the body and a piece of elastic.

Activity

The children create different shapes by stretching loops of elastic with their body parts (toes, head, arms, legs).

Procedure

Give each child a loop of elastic. The children work independently, using the elastic loops to create a variety of shapes such as a square, a rectangle, a triangle. One child may lie on the floor to create a triangle, another may kneel to create a square. After they have explored different geometric shapes, ask them to create still other shapes by using their loops and stretching their bodies into new positions at different levels. When they have developed some facility using the loops with their bodies, play a drum. As you tap the drum, they move their bodies and stretch the elastic loops into a new position. When the drum beats stop, they freeze in position and enjoy the various shapes they have created. Repeat.

*Supplementary Activity

Have the children (two at a time) share their elastic loops to create different shapes. The two children may hold their own loops while stretching their bodies into each other's loops. You may later want to have four to six children share one large loop of elastic to create interesting shapes.

Materials

A loop of elastic approximately 2 yds. in length and ¼″ or ⅜″ in width for each child

*One large loop of elastic approximately 7 yds. in length and 1″ in width

Body Language

The children move their body parts creatively to gesture to others.

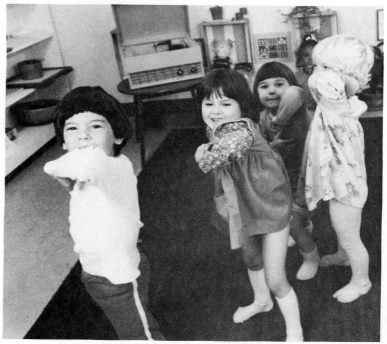

Activity

The children use their body parts in creative ways to communicate ideas such as "look up there," "hello, good to see you," and "please come and join me."

Procedure

Select a spot on the ceiling or wall, or some object in the room, and ask the children to point at it with their hands. Then ask them to point at it with their elbows. Challenge them to point with other body parts (knee, shoulder, head, both hands, foot, toe, nose).

Ask the children to show you how they use a body part to wave to a friend. Then invite them to try creative ways to use other body parts for waving. Make certain each child has an opportunity to share with the others some unique way to wave to a friend using a body part other than the hand.

Finally, have the children show you how to beckon with the hand for somebody to come to them. Use the procedure suggested above to encourage the children to use different body parts. You may want to include other body gestures in the activity such as "go away," "look down here," "he went that way."

*Supplementary Activity

Play the recording "Slow Jazz Patterns" and permit the children to move freely to the music. Then suggest they do a dance to the music that includes body part gestures. They could do a "pointing dance" such as: point four times (four beats) with the hand, four times with the elbow, four times with the knee, and four times with the foot. The music is 32 measures long (four beats to the measure), which means they can do the whole pattern eight times. Other dances could be planned using gestures for waving, beckoning, or a combination of pointing, waving, and beckoning. Encourage the children to move their bodies creatively while dancing. They may eventually make up their own pointing dance.

Materials

*Phonograph
Recording of "Slow Jazz Patterns"

Drama
Activities

Witches' Soup

The children create a witch role.

Activity

The children pantomime making and eating a witches' soup, then create a witch role.

Procedure

Make a circle (approximately 4' in diameter) on the floor with chalk, string, or masking tape, and have the children sit around it. Tell them to imagine that the circle is a big pot filled with bubbly hot water into which they will put things to make a witches' soup. They may want to pantomime placing a finger or hand in the pot, showing how hot the water is.

Ask them to add anything they want to the soup, naming the item as they do so. An old shoe, a tooth, dandruff, loose hair, leaves, sticks, rusty cans, banana skins, plastic wrappers, feathers, crayons, clipped fingernails, may be appropriate for a witches' soup. Encourage them to think of creative ways to pantomime placing the items in the pot. And every good soup-maker stirs the soup!

When the soup is ready to eat and they have all revealed how hungry they are, have them one by one use their spoons to dip into the pot and taste the soup. Eventually they all begin eating. After a period of eating and enjoying the soup, they begin to walk and talk like a witch. They may even decide to have indigestion. Comment and ask questions throughout the activity to encourage creative pantomiming.

Supplementary Activity

Invite the children to make another kind of soup: a magic soup that when eaten will let people turn into anything they want. Use the same procedure to make the soup, but this time include different ingredients. After eating the soup, the children name then role-play what the magic soup has turned them into (such as a flower, bicycle, giant, ant, airplane, snake, chicken, monkey, clown, policeman, ice-cream man).

Materials

Masking tape, chalk, or string

Walking Barefoot

The children move creatively to illustrate ways of walking.

Activity

The children move creatively to illustrate how walking barefoot on (or in) a variety of surfaces might look.

Procedure

Involve the children in a discussion about the different kinds of surfaces they might have walked on (or in) while barefooted (sand, wood, concrete, mud, rocks, etc.). Let volunteers demonstrate what they looked like while walking. Eventually, involve all the children in imitative walking of the volunteer models.

Next, invite the children one by one to demonstrate how they might walk on (or in) surfaces such as hot sand, ice, a slippery floor, mud, 3" of water at the beach or lake, a waterbed, a soft rug or mat, a wooden floor with splinters, rocks, silly putty, glue or paste, wire or rope, etc. Encourage them to move imaginatively, using their entire bodies when possible. Help the children decide who presented the most convincing walks for the different surfaces. Ask why some children were convincing.

*Supplementary Activity

Have the children walk freely in the room on (or in) a surface you name. For instance, you may say "mud," and the children walk until you give one loud tap on a drum. At the sound of the drum beat they freeze. You call out another surface such as "ice." They then move until your next drum beat, and so on. They should change direction for each new surface.

Materials

*Drum with beater

Ice Cream Shop

The children create roles associated with a place. (See page xv for special instructions.)

Activity

The children pantomime actions, improvise dialog, and create roles associated with an ice cream shop.

Procedure

Discuss with the children either what they have seen or anticipate seeing in an ice cream shop. Ask them to imagine the layout: counter, tubs of different flavored ice cream, door, cash register, tables and chairs, rubbish can, etc.

First, ask all the children to pantomime scooping ice cream, putting it into a cone, then eating it. Then have the group pantomime actions typical of an ice cream shop: making cones, cleaning the counter, sweeping the floor, wiping tables, making change at the cash register, throwing out empty ice cream tubs, bringing in new tubs filled with ice cream, cleaning hands with a napkin, eating ice cream in a cone and in a dish. Ask a few children at a time to role-play, with dialog, a brief scene one might see in an ice cream shop. Comment and ask questions to encourage creative dialog and role-playing. We recommend you repeat this activity on another day.

Supplementary Activity

Use similar procedures to help the children create other places such as a toy store, an airplane, a popcorn stand at a theater, a zoo. Encourage originality by asking questions that will help the children think of different ways to role-play actions and create dialog.

Nursery Rhyme Dramatizations

The children create dramatizations of nursery rhymes.

Activity

The children dramatize characters and actions suggested by nursery rhymes.

Procedure

Select one of the nursery rhymes below (or another of your choice) for a dramatization activity. You may want to read the rhyme to the children several times and eventually have them memorize it. When they are familiar with the selected rhyme, ask questions to help them discover its characters and actions. Volunteers can portray a character and/or action. For instance, in "The Crooked Sixpence" a child might dramatize a "crooked" man and a "straight" man. Another child might dramatize a crooked cat, another a crooked mouse, etc. After children have shared their portrayals of characters and actions, have them help you plan a group dramatization of the rhyme. Individual children may do character and/or action parts, or the children as a group may dramatize all the characters and actions. Ask questions throughout the activity to stimulate original ideas.

The Mulberry Bush

Here we go round the mulberry bush,
The mulberry bush, the mulberry bush,
Here we go round the mulberry bush,
On a cold and frosty morning.

This is the way we wash our hands,
Wash our hands, wash our hands,
This is the way we wash our hands,
On a cold and frosty morning.

This is the way we wash our clothes,
Wash our clothes, wash our clothes,
This is the way we wash our clothes,
On a cold and frosty morning.

This is the way we go to school
Go to school, go to school,
This is the way we go to school,
On a cold and frosty morning.

This is the way we come out of school,
Come out of school, come out of school,
This is the way we come out of school,
On a cold and frosty morning.

The Crooked Man

There was a crooked man, and he
    went a crooked mile,
He found a crooked sixpence
    beside a crooked stile;
He bought a crooked cat, which
    caught a crooked mouse,
And they all lived together in a
    little crooked house.

The Little Bird

Once I saw a little bird
    Come hop, hop, hop;
So I cried, "Little Bird,
    Will you stop, stop, stop?"

And was going to the window
    To say, "How do you do?"
But he shook his little tail,
    And far away he flew.

The Cat and the Fiddle

(dramatized in photograph on previous page)

Hey, diddle, diddle!
The cat and the fiddle,
The cow jumped over the moon;
The little dog laughed
To see such sport,
And the dish ran away with the spoon.

Supplementary Activity

Follow the procedure with other rhymes, and repeat this kind of activity several times during the school year.

Noah's Ark

The children create animal roles and improvise dialog.

Activity

The children eat magic animal crackers then move creatively to role-play animals; they also improvise dialog.

Procedure

Use masking tape to outline a boat with gangplank on the floor. Ask the children to sit around the outline as you tell them a brief story about Noah's ark. Tell the children they will be going on board the ship as one of Noah's animals. But first they will need to eat some magic animal crackers. Give each child an animal cracker to eat; they may become the animal they have eaten, or another animal of their choice. You should demonstrate this by eating a cracker, moving and making sounds like the animal you have eaten, then imitating that animal.

When the children have eaten their crackers, ask them to move around the room and make sounds like the animals they have eaten. You might need to side coach them: "How does your animal sleep?" "How does your animal clean itself?" "What kind of food does it eat?" "Is your animal big and heavy or thin and light?" "What kind of sound does your animal make?" "How does your animal play?" Challenge the children to role-play their animals in convincing ways. Next, have them line up to board the boat. As they go up the gangplank, stimulate dialog by asking: "Where would you like to be in the ark?" "How often do you need to be fed?" "Would you like to know where the food and water are on the boat?" "What other animals would you like to be near on the boat?" Once all the animals are on board and settled, the rain begins and off they go on their adventure.

Supplementary Activity

Extend the activity by having children create sounds to enliven the boat adventure: wind, rain, and waves. The animals in the boat could pantomime the boat's motion as it rolls back and forth with the wind and waves. The rolling motion finally subsides, and the animals all settle into sleep on calm water to end the adventure.

Materials

Masking tape
Animal crackers

Props

The children use props in creative ways.

Activity

The children select props to use creatively either individually or with a partner.

Procedure

Show the children several props such as an umbrella, a piece of rope, an empty paper towel tube. Suggest creative ways the props might be used. For instance, the cardboard tube could be a spy glass, horn, megaphone, cookie cutter. The umbrella could be a rocket ship (folded), helicopter, jelly fish, parachute. The piece of rope could be a snake, long noodle, leash for a puppy. Ask the children to select props and either independently or with a partner use them in as many different ways as possible. They may use dialog or pantomime as they present their props. Give recognition to children who are imaginative and discover a variety of interesting uses for the props.

*Supplementary Activity

The activity may be extended by having the children use one new prop (toy shovel, toy bucket, dowel stick, waste basket, chair, etc.) to do something interesting and different.

Materials

Umbrella, piece of rope, empty paper towel tube

*Other possible items: trash can lid, broomstick, spool of thread, empty clorox bottle, clothespin, tire, pots and pans, toy shovel, toy bucket, dowel stick, waste basket, chair.

Hatching Creatures

The children use pantomime to create imaginary creatures.

Activity

The children imagine they are unborn creatures in an egg, and pantomime the hatching process.

Procedure

Ask three to seven children to sit in a circle. Tell them to imagine they are some kind of creature inside an egg, ready to hatch. They can kneel, stand, lie flat on the floor, crunch themselves up, or take any position they choose. As you play ten beats on a drum (or clap your hands for twenty beats), ask the children to pantomime creatures gradually breaking through eggshells. As they begin moving, suggest they close their eyes to concentrate. As the creatures are hatching, comment on their progress. Especially make comments to children who are doing creative things with their bodies. For example, "Oh look, here is a different kind of creature" (student has twisted into an unusual form). "I wonder what kind of creature this will be after hatching." When the children hatch from their eggs, they are to freeze. Ask the children one at a time to share their creatures. Each child might also show how his or her creature eats, sleeps, cleans itself, etc. When all children have shown their creatures, repeat the hatching process to grow new creatures.

Supplementary Activity

Have the children create a zoo of creatures (each in a separate cage). You may act as a zoo keeper or a visitor who comments about the creatures.

Materials

Drum with beater (optional)

Hat Characters

The children role-play characters suggested by hats, and improvise dialogs.

Activity

The children select hats to wear, assume the characters suggested by the hats, and improvise dialogs with each other.

Procedure

Invite the children to select hats they would like to wear. Help them identify the roles of the persons who might wear their hats. After they are able to identify the characters suggested by the hats, have them move around the room and talk as the assumed characters. For instance, the "police officer" might talk with the "nurse" about how she hurt herself; the "king" might plan with the "clown" for entertainment for his guests; the "baseball player" might tell the "fire fighter" about the game her team recently won; the "pirate" might talk with the "construction worker" about building a new boat. Take an active part in helping the children develop their characters by asking questions that will prompt discovery and imagination. After awhile, the children can exchange hats, assume new characters, and again improvise dialog with each other.

Supplementary Activity

After the children have had some experience role-playing the different characters and improvising dialogs, you might assist them in creating their own short scenes that involve three or four different characters.

Materials

Large box of different kinds of hats (hats children bring from home; old hats acquired from public relations officers for city, state, and federal agencies; hats donated by different individuals; hats made from construction paper, etc.)

Hands and Feet Stories

The children use their hands and feet in creative ways to tell stories.

Activity

The children use their hands and feet to create brief stories that describe specific activities and events.

Procedure

Turn a table on its side. Kneel behind it explaining to the children that you are going to tell a brief story using (showing) only your hands. For instance, pantomime conducting a band. Your hands could suddenly stop the band and point to band members who are playing off the beat. After correcting the performance, start the band and continue to conduct for a brief time. After you finish, discuss with the children their observations of what happened.

To further explore the idea of telling a story with hands, have all the children tell a brief story as you coach them through the various events. They could tell a story about holding a book and turning the pages one by one. A pesky mosquito disturbs a child, who puts down the book and swats the pest with the hands. Eventually have one child at a time go behind the table and create a story using only the hands (peeling an orange, washing clothes, cooking foods, two spiders battling each other, playing with silly putty, playing cards, etc.).

Next, in a similar procedure, have them go behind the suspended sheet to tell stories with their feet (running, walking in mud, walking on hot sand, mosquito bites that make itchy feet, picking up objects with the toes, tip-toe movements, stomping mean pests, etc.). Encourage originality in their pantomimes.

Supplementary Activity

See *Guess What I Am Doing* activity. Have the children take turns using their hands and feet behind the table and sheet to create brief actions that the others are to identify (lacing boots, stepping over objects, shining shoes, applying nail polish to fingernails, cutting meat or vegetables, sewing, etc.).

Materials

Table, approximately 4' x 2½'
Sheet (suspended)
Clothesline and pins

Telephone Talk

The child improvises a telephone dialog.

Activity

The child uses a toy or make-believe telephone to improvise a dialog with an imaginary person.

Procedure

Engage a child in a conversation on a toy or a make-believe telephone. You might ask questions to prompt dialog. Use the child's comments as a starter to help him or her improvise an interesting dialog with you.

Then ask the child to telephone somebody of interest (family member, friend, fireman, toy shop worker, teacher, doctor, ice cream person, etc.). The child pantomimes dialing the number, then begins a dialog by identifying the person called. You may need to side coach by offering suggestions. For instance, encouraging him or her to ask questions, answer imaginary questions, tell about a past or future activity, express different moods with tone (happy, sad, angry), describe school, tell about an interesting friend. To start the child, you may need to role-play the person called. Prompt the child to stimulate original ideas and interesting dialog.

Supplementary Activity

Ask the child to select a friend in the group to talk with on the telephone. Both children should have completed the above activity. Side coach the children when necessary to help them maintain a consistent flow of creative dialog.

Materials

Toy telephone(s) (optional)

Mechanical Toy Shop

The children create a role as they pantomime mechanical toy movements.

Activity

The children observe a variety of moving mechanical toys then pantomime those movements.

Procedure

Have the children sit in a circle, and show them the different mechanical toys you have collected. Make the toys move, one by one, and ask the children to observe closely the movements. Invite the children to describe other mechanical toys and the kinds of movements they have seen.

Show a wind-up toy with a key in the back, wind it up, and let the toy move. Then have half the group imagine they are wind-up toys, while the other half turn imaginary keys in their backs to "wind them up." The children role-playing toys will begin to pantomime movements after they are wound up. Later have the two groups exchange roles.

Invent a brief story to tell the children about a toy shop in which all the toys come alive at midnight and begin to move. When the rooster crows at sunrise, all the toys suddenly "freeze" so their magic will not be discovered. All the children, or children in small groups, can try out the story plan. At the bell (sound source) for midnight, the children become mechanical toys of their choice; they continue to move like toys until the signal of a crowing rooster (sound source) at sunrise. You may become actively involved in the story plan as toy maker, shop keeper, or toy repair person.

*Supplementary Activity

Invite the children to become different types of mechanical toys (wind-up and battery-operated). Play the recording "Mechanical Toy Music," and tell the children to move only when they hear music. When the music stops, they freeze until the music begins again. Stop and start the music by raising and lowering the phonograph needle, or by using the pause switch (if the phonograph has one). Encourage imaginative, mechanical-like movements by the "toys."

Materials

Sound source for bell sound.
A variety of wind-up and battery-operated toys and dolls

*Phonograph
Recording of "Mechanical Toy Music"

Emotions

The children creatively express emotions with their faces, arms, and hands.

Activity

The children place their faces, arms, and hands in openings of a cardboard frame to creatively express a variety of emotions.

Procedure

Ask the children if you can tell whether people are happy or sad if they do not talk about it. Invite volunteers to pantomime happy and sad expressions. Lead them to discover that facial expressions and the way people move may reveal how they feel. Suggest that other emotions may be expressed without talking: surprise, excitement, anticipation, fear, anger, being lost, hunger, thirst, etc.

Have the children one by one go behind the sheet of cardboard, placing face and arms through the openings. They express a particular emotion on your signal. You may say "anger," and the child shows with face, arms, and hands that expression. Follow the same procedure for other emotions, permitting each child several opportunities to share his or her expressions with the others. Encourage them to make their expressions unique.

Supplementary Activity

Have the children as a group again express emotions, without the cardboard sheet. As you call out an emotion they use their faces and entire bodies (they may even move about the room) to express it. Have the children pause at times to watch any child who creates a convincing portrayal of an emotion.

Materials

4' x 4' sheet of cardboard or heavy paper with a 12" circular hole (for the face) and two 6" circular holes (for the arms)

Line, rope, or some other means of supporting or suspending the cardboard sheet

Caged Animals

The children create roles as they pantomime animals.

Activity

The children create roles by pantomiming the behavioral characteristics of caged animals at a zoo.

Procedure

This activity is best undertaken following a visit to a local zoo, although this is not necessary.

After the cage wall is assembled and hung on a rope, go behind the "bars" and pantomime an animal the children will recognize (monkey, lion, bear). Make sounds and pantomime moving, sleeping, eating, cleaning, playing, and generally behaving as the animal would behave. Before asking the children to name the animal, ask questions that will cause them to think and use their imaginations: "Is the animal light or heavy? Big or small? How could you tell? Does the animal move slow or fast? Is the animal gentle or rough?"

When the children understand this approach, have them take turns going into the cage and becoming animals of their choice. If a child has difficulty getting started, ask questions similar to those above. You could become involved with the animal by acting as the zoo caretaker or as a visitor who feeds the animal and takes pictures of it. Excite the watchers' imaginations by asking: "Do you think I could pet this animal? What should I feed this animal? Would this animal make a good pet to keep in the house?" Should some children wish to go into the cage and pantomime an animal with a friend, encourage them. Two children acting together could even develop a plot for their animal pantomimes.

Supplementary Activity

Invite the children to go on an "animal walk." One child is selected to pantomime a particular animal and create a role the others will imitate. After a brief animal walk, another child pantomimes a different animal and creates a role to be imitated, and so on.

Materials

Four 6' x 6" cardboard strips
Cloth strips (nonraveling fabric)
Heavy cord or rope

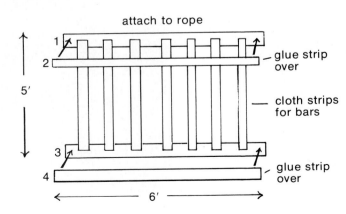

Body Sculptures

The children create human body sculptures.

Activity

The children create body sculptures: one child assumes the role of sculptor, another the role of clay.

Procedure

Ask one child to help you demonstrate this activity. Tell the children your helper will be your "lump of clay." Demonstrate how to pull, bend, and twist your clay to create a human body sculpture. After you have created a sculpture and the children have enjoyed it, have them work in pairs to create their own sculptures. One child will be the sculptor and the other a lump of clay. Remind them that once the clay is put into shape, it stays in the shape, or position, until the sculptor again moves the clay. Encourage them to make their sculptures as interesting as possible. Eventually have them exchange roles.

*Supplementary Activity

Show the children pictures of sculptures in which the statues touch each other. Then group the children by fours—one child to be sculptor, the other three to be lumps of clay. The sculptor must create a sculpture using all his lumps of clay, and the lumps must touch each other in some interesting way. Encourage the childen to work fast, thinking in terms of levels as they work. For instance, a sculpture may include one statue standing, one kneeling, and one lying flat.

Materials

*Several pictures of sculptures (including statues that touch each other)

Walking Patterns

The children move creatively to pantomime walking patterns of people and animals.

Activity

The children assume roles and move creatively to pantomime the walking patterns of people and animals.

Procedure

Involve the children in a discussion about the different ways people and animals walk. They may respond instantaneously by wanting to role-play those they name. Invite the children as a group to walk and role-play the following: duck, elephant, baby, muscleman, drunk, giant, lion, and others. Ask questions as they move to help them concentrate on their roles. "Does a duck move up and down or from side to side?" "Does an elephant move quickly or slowly?" "Does a baby sometimes fall down or stumble when trying to walk? What does the baby do with hands and arms?" "Does a giant stand tall when walking?" Encourage them to move their bodies expressively as they pantomime walking patterns.

*Supplementary Activity

Show the children a picture of a person or an animal not included in the activity. They may, for instance, look at a picture of a business person dressed up and carrying a briefcase, then as a group role-play that walking pattern. The next picture might be of a snake. They pantomime as a group the snake's movements, then follow the same procedure for other pictures such as an ant, a wrestler, and so on.

Materials

*Assorted pictures of people and animals cut from magazines and newspapers

Guess Where I Am

The children create roles associated with different places.

Activity

The children are given cards with pictures of different places; they take turns creating roles associated with the places.

Procedure

Select and name a place familiar to the children in your locality (swimming pool, ice cream store, bath tub, sand box, etc.). Have them pantomime being in that place. Then pass out the cards with pictures of different places. Each child (or children in pairs) keeps the picture hidden from the others. Invite the children to take turns pantomiming actions associated with the places in their pictures. Those who watch should not guess until the child (children) finishes. Encourage originality and make suggestions that will stimulate creative thought. This activity should be repeated on another day with different places.

Supplementary Activity

Show a new picture and ask the children to pantomime—as a group—actions associated with the place identified. Encourage them to watch each other and identify those most convincing in their pantomimes. Have them later say why they felt some were more convincing.

Materials

Cards—one for each child or for pairs of children—with pictures or drawings of places they will recognize (space ship, seesaw, airplane, ladder, tunnel, zoo, under water, football game, merry-go-round, beach, snow, tree, dinner table, etc.)

Guess What I'm Wearing

The children creatively pantomine putting on articles of clothing.

Activity

The children present creative pantomimes of dressing.

Procedure

Tell the children you are going to pantomime putting on an article of clothing and they are to identify what you have put on. You might begin with slacks, socks, or shoes. Next, put on a hat. Gradually involve the children by asking them one by one to briefly pantomime putting on an article of clothing. The children watching should not guess until each pantomime has been completed. After all the children have pantomimed, ask them again to take turns presenting longer pantomimes. This time they put on two articles of clothing (underwear, slacks, dresses, socks, shoes, shirts, coats, gloves, hats, belts, etc.). Encourage them to take sufficient time to be convincing. After each child finishes, the others identify the articles of clothing put on.

Supplementary Activity

You might extend the activity by having the children pantomime other actions typical of somebody getting ready to go somewhere: bathing, shining shoes, ironing clothes, spraying deodorant, brushing teeth, combing hair, putting on lipstick, trimming toenails, etc. They then put on articles of clothing, and later trim fingernails, paint fingernails, put on jewelry, brush lint off clothes, look in mirror, put on powder, etc. The children watching should later identify all actions pantomimed.

Guess What I'm Riding

The children move creatively as they pantomime riding in or on different kinds of transportation.

Activity

The children name different kinds of transportation; they then move creatively to pantomime riding in or on them.

Procedure

Ask the children to name different kinds of transportation on, or in which, they either have, or could, ride (car, wagon, roller skates, surf board, skate board, scooter, airplane, motorcycle, tricycle, merry-go-round, horse, etc.). When they have named as many as they can, invite them as a group to creatively pantomime riding them. They may make sounds to represent the transportation, or move to reveal the motion of a person riding in or on that transportation. They may eventually present their pantomimes singly or in pairs. Encourage the children to closely observe each pantomime and identify those most interesting and convincing.

Supplementary Activity

Select one child to be leader for a follow-the-leader game. The leader calls out a kind of transportation, such as "horse," then pantomimes a horse trotting or galloping. The others follow with their own horse pantomimes. After a brief period, the leader will call out another kind of transportation such as "airplane," and so on. Let different children have a turn as leader. Encourage each child to move creatively, not to attempt an exact replication of the leader's movements.

Guess What I'm Eating

The children create a role as they pantomime eating foods.

Activity

The children are given picture cards of different foods. They take turns pantomiming eating the food identified as the other children guess the food.

Procedure

Select foods familiar to the children in your locality: spaghetti, hamburger, ice cream cone, soup, apple, orange, peanuts, banana, corn on the cob, licorice or taffy, and hard-boiled egg may be appropriate. Name one food and have them pantomime eating it.

Pass out the cards with pictures of food. Each child should keep his or her picture hidden from the others. Invite the children to take turns to pantomime eating the food pictured. They should take time to adequately use their hands, fingers, and mouths, and improvise eating sounds. They might also try to reveal whether the food is hot or cold. Children watching should not guess until the child finishes. Repeat the activity on another day with different foods.

Supplementary Activity

The children can take turns pantomiming eating an entire meal using utensils and drinking a beverage. Ask the children to identify those most convincing in their pantomimes and tell why.

Materials

Index cards with pictures or drawings of familiar foods (one for each child)

Guess What I'm Doing

The children create roles as they pantomime work and play activities.

Activity

The children are given picture cards of different work and play activities. They take turns pantomiming the activity identified as the others guess what they are doing.

Procedure

Select activities familiar to the children in your locality, such as working as dentist-patient, beauty shop operator-customer, cooking, playing baseball, playing dodgeball, swimming, washing clothes by hand, riding a tricycle. Name one activity and have the children as a group pantomime it.

Pass out the cards with pictures of activities. Each child (or pair) keeps the picture hidden from the others. The children take turns pantomiming the activity pictured. They should take time to adequately use their bodies, and make sounds that will help the others identify what they are doing. Those watching withhold their guesses until the child (children) completes the pantomime. This can be repeated on another day with different activities.

Supplementary Activity

Show a new picture and have the children as a group pantomime the activity. Ask the children to identify those most convincing in their pantomimes.

Materials

Index cards with pictures or drawings of a familiar work or play activity (one for each child or for pairs of children)

Art
Activities

Crazy Wigs

The children create wigs.

Activity

The children create wigs by attaching newspaper strips to a basic form.

Procedure

Ask the children to look at each other's hair, noticing differences. Show pictures, if available, of people with different kinds of hair and hair styles. Tell the children that they will create wigs and may choose any hair style they wish. Show them a basic wig form and the newspaper strips. You may need to make a wig first, to show them how to attach newspaper strips to the form with staples or glue. Begin attaching strips at the bottom edge of the form, and gradually add other strips as you work your way to the top. Show later how to trim the wig, add flowers or other items, even a hat.

   Next, give each child a basic form and make available the variety of newspaper strips. Lend assistance as necessary. Later, when the wigs are completed, invite the children one by one to model their wigs for the others.

*Supplementary Activity

Give the children a basic wig form, and invite them to create another wig using assorted strips of cloth, string, yarn, and other available materials. A "fashion show" will provide the children an opportunity to model their creations.

Materials

Pictures showing a variety of hair types and styles

Old manila folders or similar heavy paper to make a basic wig form for each child

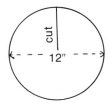 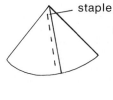 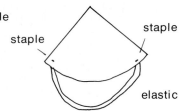

Newspaper cut into a variety of strips:

*Cloth scraps cut into a variety of strips
  Assorted materials such as string, yarn, heavy cord

Rainbow Colors

The child uses primary colors to create a variety of secondary colors.

Activity

The child uses tongue depressors to put primary colors in empty containers; he or she mixes colors in equal and unequal proportions to create a variety of secondary colors.

Procedure

Give the child the box with the different materials listed below. With tongue depressors, he or she puts equal amounts of two of the colors in an empty container, then mixes the colors with a brush to see what new color has been created. The child continues to experiment by varying the proportions of primary colors in empty containers (for example, one proportion of blue to four of yellow will produce the color chartreuse). Later invite the child to paint a picture using some of the colors created.

*Supplementary Activity

The children experiment individually with different proportions of black and white to create a variety of shades and pastels. They may later wish to paint a picture using some of the colors created. It is important that only a tiny proportion of black be added to another color; a larger proportion of white will be needed to change other colors.

Materials

Box (approximate size to hold the materials)
Several empty plastic containers
Tempera paint (red, yellow, blue)
Tongue depressors or popsicle sticks
Brushes
Paper

*Tempera paint (black, white)

Balloon Sculpture

The child creates a balloon sculpture.

Activity

The child uses two-way tape and assorted colors of small balloons to create a balloon sculpture.

Procedure

Give the child the small balloons to play with for a few minutes. Later show how to use two-way tape to stick the balloons together. Then invite him or her to create a balloon sculpture using two-way tape and all the balloons: a representational object, a design, or abstract form of some kind. You might later ask the child to describe what was created, to stimulate imaginative thought and prompt dialog. We recommend that this activity be repeated on another day with assorted sizes of balloons, and that the child be allowed to take the balloon sculptures home.

*Supplementary Activity

Invite the child to create another sculpture, fastening additional objects to the balloons. Each balloon in the sculpture could have a face, the balloons together could become one person or animal, the sculpture could become a representational object, etc. Ask questions and comment as the child works to stimulate creative thought. When he or she finishes, ask what has been created.

Materials

Two-way transparent tape

Assorted colors of small inflated balloons (about twelve balloons per child; to prevent popping, do not inflate completely)

*Assorted buttons, cut-out paper designs, cloth shapes, other objects
 Assorted sizes of balloons

T-shirt Designing

The children create T-shirt designs.

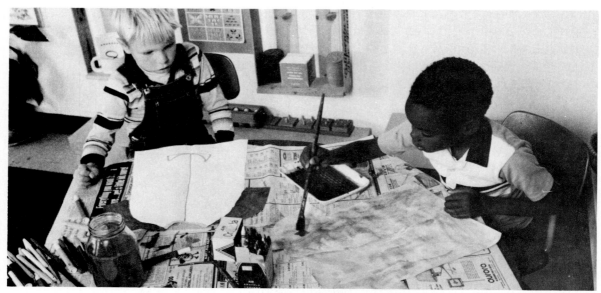

Activity

The children create T-shirt designs on paper shirt patterns.

Procedure

Ask the children to look at various T-shirt designs, either on T-shirts they are wearing or on some you have available. Help them be aware of designs that include words, pictures, art work, or some combination of the three.

Give each child a T-shirt pattern and provide crayons, pencils, felt-tip pens, paints, and brushes. Invite them to decorate the T-shirt patterns, encouraging them to think BIG as they create designs. When they complete their designs and the paints are dry, have them cut the T-shirts from the sheet of paper, and "wear" them by fastening them onto their clothes with safety pins. A fashion show to model the T-shirt designs could be an enjoyable experience for them.

*Supplementary Activity

Ask the children to bring from home old plain white or pastel-colored T-shirts on which to paint designs. Have them use acrylic paints (dilute with water: one part paint to three parts water), which will be permanent after drying. They should put newspapers inside the torso and sleeves of the shirt before they begin to paint. Again, encourage them to think BIG. When they complete their work, ask them to remove the newspapers, and hang up the shirts to dry. A fashion show for a parent's gathering might be fun for both the children and parents.

Materials

Paper T-shirt pattern, approximately 18" x 24" (based on Master No. 4 in the Appendix)
Paints
Felt-tip pens
Crayons
Pencils
Brushes
Scissors
Safety pins
Newspapers

*Acrylic paints

Rock Art

The children create designs on rocks.

Activity

The children use acrylic paints to create original designs on smooth rocks.

Procedure

Give each child a smooth rock. Ask them to look at and feel the shapes and surfaces of the rocks. Then ask that they look again to imagine what kind of design they might paint on their rocks to make them interesting.

Make the materials available, and invite the children to begin painting their rocks. As they work, ask questions that will encourage originality. Suggest that their completed creations be used as gifts for special friends or relatives.

*Supplementary Activity

Obtain one or more large rocks (smooth or jagged), and invite the children to create a "rock mural." Each child will paint one or more designs on the rock, which may later be displayed at an evening program for parents. An extension of the activity is to glue (crazy glue or super glue) smaller rocks together to create a rock formation for another "rock mural."

Materials

Smooth rocks (one for each child; you might encourage the children to bring rocks from home)
Assorted acrylic paints
Brushes

*One or more large rocks (smooth or jagged)
 Crazy glue or super glue (recommended use ONLY by teacher)
 Assorted small rocks (smooth or jagged)

Film Making

The children create an art film.

Activity

The children create an art film by drawing on film leader with felt-tip pens.

Procedure

Give the children drawing paper and felt-tip pens, and ask them to draw small wavy lines, small zigzag lines, a variety of small shapes, dots, etc. When they have enjoyed drawing and sharing their work with each other, show them the roll of leader film. Tell them that after they draw some of their favorite lines and shapes on the film, they will then see their "art movie" projected on a screen.

Place newspapers on the floor, unroll the leader film on the newspapers, and help each child find an area in which to work. So the children can recognize their own efforts, space them so that a blank section (approximately 3") is left between each child's work. Encourage them to use all space on the film assigned to them. Later, show the children their "art movie." The film may be appropriate for showing during an evening program for parents, perhaps with background music.

Supplementary Activity

Have some of the more-experienced children create another art film that includes repeated simple shapes and drawings. This will result in a kind of animation. An activity in which all children might participate is to project the art film onto a sheet as children move underneath it, creating forms and shapes (see *Sheet and Body Sculptures* activity).

Materials

Drawing paper
Felt-tip pens of assorted colors (with ink that will transfer to acetate or a glossy surface)
Film projector (16 mm recommended; 8 mm usable)
Screen or white wall for projection
One roll of leader film for the size of the projector available
Old newspapers

Three-Dimensional Collages

The children use three-dimensional objects to create collages.

Activity

The children use a variety of three-dimensional objects to create designs or abstract or representational collages.

Procedure

The children should have completed the *Thematic Collages* activity (p. 102) prior to this activity.

Ask the children to look at the variety of materials collected, and observe you as you create a simple collage (design, abstract, or representational). Be certain to rearrange the items you select in different patterns so the children will understand the need to try out ideas before making decisions. When you are satisfied with the arrangement, glue the items in position on a sheet of 9" x 12" paper.

Invite the children to create collages. Help them select themes such as at the beach, at the zoo, my fish tank. Asking questions such as "What do you see at the beach?" "What do you see at the zoo?" will motivate them and stimulate creative thought. Continue to ask questions as they work to encourage originality and use of imagination.

*Supplementary Activity

The activity may be extended by having the children include in their collages pictures and shapes cut from magazines. They also could draw or paint pictures and designs to add more variety. When they finish, encourage them to share their work with each other.

Materials

Variety of geometric and other shapes cut from materials such as aluminum foil, sandpaper, screen, fabric, felt
Sheet of heavy-weight paper (approximately 9" x 12")
Scissors
Glue with brushes
Assorted three-dimensional items such as toothpicks, yarn scraps, plastic and paper straws, leaves, tiny pebbles, buttons, lace, rickrack, seeds, pods, bottle caps, balsa wood strips, feathers
Assorted paints and felt-tip pens

*Variety of pictures and shapes cut from magazines

Wire Sculptures

The children create three-dimensional wire sculptures.

Activity

The children use wire and other materials to create three-dimensional objects.

Procedure

Create a three-dimensional sculpture with wire as the children observe the operation. You may want to add nuts, bolts, washers, beads, or other items to enhance the sculpture. The sculpture can be mounted on a block of wood or a piece of styrofoam or clay after it has been completed.

Give the children materials to create a wire sculpture. They may wish to make an animal, person, object, puppet, or a form of some kind. Particularly, help them understand they are to create a three-dimensional shape. As the children work, ask questions that will arouse their curiosity and cause them to think of alternatives.

Supplementary Activity

As a follow-up, invite the children to create three-dimensional sculptures to later be displayed for parents and other groups of children in the school. Select a theme such as creature zoo, animals, interesting things, toys, playground, airplanes, carnival. Encourage originality by asking the children questions that will stimulate creative thought.

Materials

Supply of pliable wire (copper wire or no. 19 stovepipe wire)
Items such as very small boxes, small blocks of wood, washers, nuts and bolts, beads

Representational Objects

The child uses paper cut into various shapes to create representational objects.

Activity

The child is given a variety of paper shapes in different colors with which to create representational objects.

Procedure

Give the child an envelope containing ten different shapes. Ask him or her to remove the shapes and select several to create something familiar. You might help the child first create a tree, then invite him or her to create another tree using some of the other shapes. Working at first to produce an image of a tree—or some other very familiar object—will encourage the child and stretch imagination. Other objects you might suggest: car, house, bird, dog. Eventually leave the child to choose a variety of objects to create. The child should later share his or her work with you and name the objects created.

*Supplementary Activity

Invite the child to create other objects using a much larger collection of different shapes in assorted colors (stored in a shoe box). A picture could be created of shapes glued on a large piece of construction paper. Encourage the child to create, if possible, a picture that tells a story. A felt-tip pen can be used to add lines to the picture for more detail.

Materials

A large envelope containing a variety of shapes in assorted colors—
   make by cutting up construction paper, Christmas wrapping paper,
   and textured wallpaper samples (large squares, small squares, rec-
   tangles, circles, triangles, and other geometric shapes)
Glue or paste

*Felt-tip pen
 A shoe box containing a much larger collection of shapes than does
   the envelope

Modified Batik Designs

The child creates a batik design.

Activity

The child uses wax and paints to create batik designs.

Procedure

We recommend that you experiment with the following procedures prior to having children create batik designs.

Prepare the work area: cover a table with newspapers, then place on the papers the wax-resist container and three containers of primary colors (red, yellow, blue). Have a brush for each container.

Invite the child to dip a brush into the wax and begin creating a design on a sheet of manila paper. When the wax is completely dry, he or she then selects a color to brush onto the paper. The child will soon recognize that the wax resists the paint, which results in a vivid design. When the paint is completely dry, more wax may be added to the design. After the wax dries, another color of paint may be added, and so on. As the primary colors overlap, secondary colors will be created. The wax and paint brushes must be cleaned with water after the batik design is completed.

*Supplementary Activity

Invite the child to further explore this art medium by drawing a design or picture on manila paper with permanent-ink felt-tip pens. Then the waxing-drying-painting-drying process may be used. The result will be a mixed media creation consisting of lines and batiking.

Materials

One container of wax resist (may be purchased from ceramic supply stores)
Caution: The wax is not to be taken internally, and you should closely monitor its use by children.
Three containers of acrylic paint (red, yellow, blue—add one part paint to five parts water)
Four brushes
Smocks or aprons (for protection against permanent paint stains)
Sheets of manila paper

*Felt-tip pens with permanent ink (assorted colors)

Cumulative Drawings

The children create cumulative drawings.

Activity

The children create cumulative drawings that may be designs, abstract, or representational.

Procedure

Before beginning this activity, children should have completed the *Scribble Creations* activity p. 122.

Draw a rectangle (approximately 18″ x 25″) on the chalkboard. Then draw a simple scribble inside the rectangle. Ask the children what the scribble looks like. After they have shared their perceptions, select one child to add more lines to the scribble. Ask another child to continue the drawing by adding still more lines, then another child, and so on. The drawing may become a design, abstract, or representational.

Following the group experience in cumulative drawing, organize the children in groups of five. Have each group sit in a circle and place felt-tip pens and crayons in the center. Give each child in each group an index card with a scribble. The children add lines to the line cues provided, and after a brief period pass their cards to the child on the right, who adds more lines. This is continued until all five children have contributed to the drawings on each of the cards. When the children receive the original cards again, they complete the drawings. Display the cards so all can enjoy them.

*Supplementary Activity

Invite the children to explore further the idea of cumulative drawing. Organize them in groups of five, and give each child a blank index card. They draw their own scribbles on the cards, then pass the cards to the right to begin the cumulative drawings.

Materials

Index cards with scribbles (one for each child)
Chalkboard and chalk
Pencils
Crayons
Felt-tip pens

*Blank index cards (one for each child)

Thematic Collages

The children use pictures cut out of magazines to create collages.

Activity

The children create thematic collages from pictures and shapes they cut out of magazines.

Procedure

Either you or the children may cut out a variety of colored pictures and shapes from magazines. When you have a large collection, choose a collage theme and demonstrate for the children how to select pictures, arrange them on a sheet of paper, and glue them to create a thematic collage. We suggest you glue the background pieces in position before gluing the foreground shapes. Then help each child choose a theme (garden, city, park, animals, people, food, etc.). Ask children to select pictures and shapes to arrange on the sheet of paper. Help the children decide arrangements by asking questions that will cause them to look, think, and use their imaginations. When the pictures are positioned, tell them to glue the pieces on the paper. Later have the children look at each other's creations and try to name the themes.

*Supplementary Activity

Invite the children to create a mural using colored pictures and shapes cut from magazines. They select a theme(s) and arrange the items in patterns on a large sheet of butcher paper, then glue them in position. Display the completed mural where all children in the school can enjoy it.

Materials

Magazines from which a variety of colored pictures and shapes may be cut
Scissors
Glue with brushes
Sheets of paper (9″ x 12″)

*Butcher paper (3′ x 6′)

Milk Carton Critters

The children create "critters" from empty milk cartons.

Activity

The children use empty milk cartons and a variety of objects to create imaginative and interesting "critters."

Procedure

Invite the children to create something new and imaginative with empty milk cartons and other objects: popsicle sticks, toothpicks, tongue depressers, feathers, Styrofoam balls, nuts and bolts, sponge, yarn, seed pods, etc. As they construct critters, ask questions and make comments to help them think in terms of alternative objects and different techniques. When the cirtters are completed, display them and encourage the children to examine each other's creations.

Supplementary Activity

Group the children by twos. Have each pair carry on an improvised dialog as they hold their critters facing each other. They might take turns asking "Who are you?" and "Why do you look like that?" etc.—encourage imaginative conversation. They exchange partners and continue the procedure as long as their interest in the activity is obvious.

Materials

Empty, clean, dry pint-sized milk cartons
Glue
Scissors
Construction paper
Box with assorted objects such as straws, buttons, beads, pipe cleaners

Yarn Mazes

The children create abstract line compositions.

Activity

The children pass yarn pieces through holes in pieces of pegboard to create abstract line compositions.

Procedure

Give the children the pegboard pieces, yarn, and plastic yarn needles. Each yarn end should be tied to the side of a paper clip to serve as a knot. You may need to tie the yarn for children who cannot do so. The children use the needles to pass pieces of yarn through the holes, letting the knot ends catch on the bottom side of the holes. They use many yarn pieces of different colors to create interesting designs. Repeat on another day so children can further develop their skills in creating abstract line compositions.

*Supplementary Activity

Invite the children to use their yarn mazes for mixed media projects. As they include items such as buttons, beads, and macaroni noodles in their yarn mazes, help them sew the items in the positions they specify. Display the creations later for all the children to enjoy.

Materials

Yarn pieces (approximately 3' long) of different colors and thicknesses
Paper clips (tied to yarn pieces to serve as knots)
Blunt-end plastic yarn needles
Scissors
Pieces of pegboard (approximately 9" x 12")

*Buttons
 Beads
 Macaroni noodles

Clay Creatures

The children create creatures from clay and assorted items.

Activity

The children shape modeling clay to use as a basic form, then add other items to the form to create clay creatures.

Procedure

Give the children the three boxes of materials and invite them to create interesting creatures. They first use clay to create a form, then add Styrofoam balls and items from the boxes. Arms, legs, heads, facial features, tails, hats, hair can thus be made. Encourage originality by suggesting that their creatures do not need arms and legs like people and animals they have seen. Completed creatures may be either kept by the children or disassembled and returned to the boxes for future use.

Supplementary Activity

The creatures created in the activity may be used to begin a "creature zoo," which will be displayed for all children in the school. The zoo could be an on-going activity where new creatures are periodically added to the collection, or new creatures are used to replace the old creatures.

Materials

Three boxes to store clay, styrofoam balls, assorted items
One bag of modeling clay
Twenty Styrofoam balls (1" to 3" in diameter)
Assorted items such as buttons, nuts and bolts, springs, pipe cleaners, bottle caps, feathers

Bird Drawings

The children create drawings of birds.

Activity

The children use a basic shape to create drawings of birds.

Procedure

Give each child a sheet of paper with a basic shape duplicated on it (Master No. 2). The children are to use the shapes to create drawings of birds in either horizontal or vertical positions. They may use pencils, crayons, and/or felt-tip pens. As the children work on their creations, closely observe their work and ask stimulating questions: "What kind of legs does your bird have? Long and skinny? Long and fat? Short and crooked?" "What kind of eyes does your bird have? Big and sad? Small and slanted?" "What kind of tail feathers? Long and colorful? Broken and sparse? Curved or straight?" "Does your bird have a long or short beak?" "Is your bird flying or sitting still?" Such questions will help the children stretch their imaginations to think of different ways to approach their bird creations.

*Supplementary Activity

Provide paper with the shape duplicated from Master No. 3. Ask the children to use their imaginations to create another drawing different from their first, this time adding more color. Later, ask them to tell you about the birds they have created.

Materials

Paper with shape duplicated from Master No. 2 (see Appendix)
Pencils
Crayons
Felt-tip pens

*Paper with shape duplicated from Master No. 3 (see Appendix)

Spray Painting

The child creates a spray-paint picture. (See page xv for special instructions.)

Activity

The child creates a picture by using cut-out shapes (negatives and positives) and spray paint.

Procedure

Use the following procedure to demonstrate how to create a spray painting.

   Place newspaper on the floor or table, a sheet of 10" x 14" cardboard on the newspaper, then a sheet of 9" x 12" paper on the cardboard. Select a cutout (positive) and pin it in a selected position on the paper. Lightly spray the cutout with paint or ink. Remove it, then pin another cutout on a separate part of the paper, or partially covering the design from the first cutout. Spray the second cutout with another color. Repeat the process with other cutouts (positives and negatives) until the picture is completed. When you feel the child understands the process, and is able to successfully use the materials, invite him or her to create a picture. Lend assistance only when necessary. Ask the child questions to stimulate imagination. Especially encourage overlapping the forms to achieve color mixing and more intricate designs.

*Supplementary Activity

Invite the child to further develop one spray-paint creation by using felt-tip pens and/or crayons for greater detail. Cutouts from designs of leaves and other objects could be added.

Materials

Three empty bottles (such as windex or plastic plant spray containers) with spray attachments for three different colors (dilute the paint one part paint to five parts water; dilute the ink one part ink to two parts water)

Ink or water-soluble poster paint (red, yellow, blue)

A wide variety of geometric and other shapes cut from scraps; save both the cutout (positives) and the sheets from which shapes have been cut (negatives)

Pins

One sheet (10" x 14") of styrofoam or cardboard

One sheet of 9" x 12" paper

Newspapers

Scissors

*Felt-tip pens
 Crayons

Snow Creatures

The children create Styrofoam sculptures.

Activity

The children use Styrofoam pellets and toothpicks to create snow creatures.

Procedure

Demonstrate for the children how to use toothpicks to connect Styrofoam pellets, creating a snow creature. After they have observed the process, invite them to create their own. Question and comment as they work to stimulate original thinking.

*Supplementary Activity

Invite the children to create new sculptures and add items such as buttons, feathers, and beads to their creations. You might have them help you create a snowy landscape as background for displaying their new snow creatures.

Materials

Assorted sizes and shapes of Styrofoam pellets (packing pellets, etc.)
Toothpicks

*Assorted items such as buttons, beads, feathers, rickrack

Body Printing

The child uses various body parts to create interesting prints.

Activity

The child uses finger paints of various colors and different body parts as printing tools to create interesting pictures and designs.

Procedure

Invite the child to the work area where the materials for the activity are prepared. Demonstrate how to use body parts as printing tools to create a picture. You might first dip the palm of your hand into one color of finger paint and make a print on a sheet of construction paper. Avoid using too much paint to prevent the different prints from dripping and running together.

   Before making another print, show the child how to rinse and wipe the paint from your palm to prevent color mixing. You might dip your thumb into another color and make two thumb prints just beneath the palm print to create legs. Next, add a print made by the side of the hand or the foot. Other body prints are added until the picture or design is complete.

   As the child begins work, encourage him or her to try making prints with many different body parts. Help with the first attempt to prepare the child for later creating a picture independently.

*Supplementary Activity

Give several children a 4′ sheet of butcher paper to create a mural consisting of body prints. Provide crayons for enhancement or detail.

Materials

Newspapers
Bowl of water
Paper towels
Bottles of finger paints stored in a box (red, yellow, blue)
Three styrofoam trays
Construction paper of any size

*Butcher paper
 Crayons

Rubbings

The children create pictures from rubbings.

Activity

The children create pictures and designs from rubbings of assorted items.

Procedure

Demonstrate for the children how to produce rubbings from items listed under **Materials**. Gradually involve the children in the process, permitting them to freely explore possibilities.

Tell the children they can now create a picture consisting of rubbings. They are to use at least five different rubbings, and decide the best placement of the rubbings (composition) in their pictures. Encourage them to think of a variety of possibilities; ask questions as they work to stimulate original thought.

*Supplementary Activity

Invite the children to create a mural of rubbings. Ask them to help you find items different from those they used in their individual pictures (plastic covers and lids, combs, brushes, parts of toys, rings and other jewelry, coins, rulers that have indentations, etc.). Help each child find a space to work; ask questions that will stimulate original ideas. Later display the mural.

Materials

Construction paper

Pencils and crayons

Items such as leaves, paper cutouts, sandpaper, tree bark, textured fabric and wallpaper, foil, cork, carpeting, screen, coins, rough boards

*Large sheet of butcher paper

Print-Making

The children create pictures and designs to use in print-making.

Activity

The children use Styrofoam sheets to create pictures and designs, which they use in print-making.

Procedure

Demonstrate for the children how to draw a picture on a Styrofoam sheet with a pencil. Then, on a smooth, flat surface such as a sheet of plexiglass, use a brayer to roll ink evenly on the Styrofoam sheet. Place a sheet of newsprint paper over the inked side of the Styrofoam sheet (block); use your hands or a spoon to rub the non-inked side of the newsprint. Be certain to rub all over the paper to produce a good print from the block. Finally, peel off the sheet of newsprint from the block and show the print you have produced. The print may be hung on a line or left lying flat on a shelf to dry.

Involve the children in creating blocks and prints. Ask questions as they work to arouse their curiosity and suggest several options. Help them see that after a block is made, it is still possible to add to the original design. They can even cut the Styrofoam block into interesting shapes, or make cuts in its center. Should the children desire to produce prints of a different color, show them how to wash their blocks and let them dry before using other colors.

Supplementary Activity

Extend the activity by having the children work in pairs or threes to produce overlapping prints on one sheet of newsprint paper. Also, they can make interesting prints by printing on a selected page from a newspaper (comic section) or a magazine. An overlapping print in different colors from the same block also produces interesting results. Encourage the children to think of creative ways to vary the print-making activity.

Materials

Two Styrofoam sheets for each child (Styrofoam trays used for packing meat and other food products are ideal; cut off the rims to make the sheet flat)
Pencils
Two or more colors of printing ink or finger paints (water soluble)
Brayers for each color
Plexiglass sheets, approximately 9" x 12"
Newspapers
Sheets of newsprint
Buckets, pans, or other containers for washing Styrofoam blocks
Paper towels for drying styrofoam plates

Scribble Creations

The children create drawings from line scribbles.

Activity

The children create abstract or representational drawings from line scribbles.

Procedure

Give each child a felt-tip pen and an index card with a simple line scribble. Ask them to imagine what the scribbles might become. By adding other lines they create a representational drawing (animal, person, object of some kind) or an abstract drawing (design of some kind). Using the scribble as a beginning, the children complete the drawing. Encourage them to be original.

*Supplementary Activity

Give the children blank index cards on which to draw a few scribble lines. Allow them only a few seconds so the scribbles will not become elaborate. Then have them exchange cards and create abstract or representational drawings from the scribbles on the new cards.

Materials

Index cards or paper cut to approximately 5" x 8", on which are drawn various line scribbles
Black felt-tip pens

*Blank index cards or cut paper

Tree Drawings

The child creates a variety of trees based on line cue drawings.

Activity

The child uses line cue drawings of tree trunks to create four different kinds of trees.

Procedure

Show the child pictures of trees, and briefly discuss some of the principal features of the different trees. Then show the line cue drawings of tree trunks, and invite him or her to add to the drawings to create four different kinds of trees. Ask questions such as "Does this tree have skinny or fat branches?" "Is this tree old? How can you tell?" "Have some of the branches been broken or sawed off?" "Are the branches crooked or straight?" "Do birds or other animals live in this tree?" "Does this tree grow fruit or nuts?" "Will this tree have leaves? Big leaves or small leaves?"

*Supplementary Activity

Prepare a large sheet of paper with a background of sky and ground. Then invite all the children to create a forest mural. They may either select trees they have already created, or create new trees to cut out and paste on the mural. Animal cutouts could be added to enliven the mural.

Materials

Pictures of various kinds of trees
Copies of line cue drawings of tree trunks (Master No. 1 in the Appendix)
Drawing paper
Felt-tip pens
Crayons

*Butcher paper
 Paste

Blot Pictures

The children create pictures from blots.

Activity

The children are given sheets of paper having two identical blots; they use felt-tip pens or crayons to create pictures from the blots.

Procedure

Fold the sheets of paper in half. On one half, squeeze two to three blobs of tempera paint. Make blobs in a variety of shapes, but keep them simple. Fold the other side of the paper and press to create two identical blot forms. Give the children felt-tip pens or crayons to create pictures from the blots. Remind them that they may use a variety of colors and heavy and light lines. Their blots could become an animal, person, creature, object, or an expression of a fantasy.

*Supplementary Activity

Use a sheet of 3' x 8' wrapping or butcher paper to create a variety of blots. Invite the children to select blots and create a mural, which they will later display in school. The mural could have a theme or simply include random pictures of interest to the children.

Materials

8½" x 11" (approximate) sheets for each child
Felt-tip pens and crayons
A variety of colors of tempera paint

*One sheet of 3' x 8' wrapping or butcher paper

Music
Activities

Stick Rhythms

The child creates a variety of rhythm patterns.

Activity

The child uses rhythm sticks to create rhythm patterns, taking turns playing with the sounds of recorded music.

Procedure

Give the child a pair of rhythm sticks; invite him or her to experiment playing the sticks loudly and softly, and to make up some rhythms. After a few minutes of exploration, play a brief, simple rhythm on another pair of sticks and have the child repeat your pattern. Continue to play other brief patterns (alternating loud and soft) for him or her to imitate.

When the child understands the procedure of "taking turns playing," play the recording "Stick Rhythms Music." The child listens to decide when to play the sticks. Encourage him or her to make up interesting parts: either loud or soft to correspond with the sounds in the recording. Give the child several opportunities to make up parts; repeat this activity on another day.

*Supplementary Activity

Invite the child to participate in a similar activity using bongo drums (other rhythm instruments can eventually be used). Encourage him or her to try different ways to play, making rhythms as unique as possible, taking turns playing with the sounds in "Stick Rhythms Music."

Materials

Phonograph
Recording of "Stick Rhythms Music"
Two pairs of rhythm sticks

*Bongo drums (two small drums of different pitch and size, attached to
   each other)

Feet Sounds Improvisation

The child creates a piece consisting of improvised feet sounds.

Activity

The child explores different sounds made with the feet, then creates a piece that includes a variety of improvised feet sounds.

Procedure

Ask the child to make as many different kinds of feet sounds as possible. He or she might experiment with walking, running, stomping, and tapping sounds while barefooted or wearing shoes or slippers. For each sound produced, the child should experiment with levels of loudness and making the sounds gradually speed up and slow down. Surfaces such as carpet, wood, grass, sand, linoleum, and concrete could be explored for a variety of sound qualities. After a period of sound exploration, the child creates and performs an improvised piece that includes some favorite feet sounds. Tape record this improvisation and play it back. The child may later want to create another improvisation as an improvement.

*Supplementary Activity

Invite the child to improvise other feet sound pieces while wearing jingle bells on the ankles or lightweight boards or other material strapped to the feet.

Materials

Cassette tape recorder

*Jingle bells
  Assorted materials that can be attached to the feet (sandpaper, plastic packing sheets, lightweight boards, etc.)

Can Sounds Composition

The child creates a piece for long and short sounds.

Activity

The child produces long and short sounds using a can and stick, devises symbols to represent the sounds, then uses the symbols to create a composition, which he or she later performs.

Procedure

Give the child an empty tin can and a rhythm stick with which to experiment how to produce long and short sounds. Tapping the can with the stick produces a short sound; placing the stick inside the can and rotating it in a circular motion produces a long sound. After the child has had time to enjoy making sounds, ask him or her to devise symbols to represent short and long sounds.   X could represent a short sound, and ⌇⌇⌇⌇ a long sound. Now the child creates and notates a piece for can and stick sounds, such as:

X ⌇⌇⌇⌇ X X X ⌇⌇⌇⌇⌇⌇⌇⌇⌇ X ⌇⌇⌇ X

Have the child practice reading the notation and playing it.

*Supplementary Activity

Make a cassette tape recording of the child's performance. Then ask him or her to make up a part to play, using a maraca, while listening to the recorded composition. If possible, record the composition with the improvised maraca part using a second cassette tape recorder. Play the new tape so the child may listen and evaluate his or her work.

Materials

Empty No. 2 tin can with the top removed (no sharp edges)
Rhythm stick
Sheet of paper
Felt-tip pen

*Cassette tape recorder
  A second cassette tape recorder (optional)
  Maraca

Santa's Sleigh Ride

The child uses jingle bells to create a sound story.

Activity

The child uses jingle bells to create a sound story about Santa's sleigh ride to deliver gifts to children.

Procedure

Give the child jingle bells and let him or her have a few minutes to play them. You might emphasize that jingle bells are often used in music, especially during the Christmas holiday season. Show the child the picture of Santa in his sleigh, and say that jingle bells are often attached to a sleigh to produce pleasing jingle sounds as animals pull it through the snow. Invite the child to make up a piece that could describe Santa's trip to deliver gifts to children. Help him or her think in terms of a sleigh beginning to move, and gradually speeding up (accelerando) until it reaches a desired speed. The sleigh continues for a brief period at a regular speed (steady beat), then begins to gradually slow down (ritardando) as Santa stops to deliver a gift. The sleigh ride sound story then resumes; the child could experiment with other speeding up and slowing down ideas as the journey continues. Tape record a performance of the sound story; play it back and let the child enjoy listening to his or her creation.

*Supplementary Activity

Ask the child to play the tone block and explore its sound capabilities. Then play the recorded sleigh ride performance, and ask him or her to play the tone block along with the jingle bell sounds to create horse hoof sounds for the sleigh ride. Record both the sleigh bell sounds and the tone block sounds using a second cassette tape recorder—play back the recording so the child may enjoy and evaluate the performance.

Materials

Picture of Santa Claus in a sleigh
Cassette tape recorder
Jingle bells

*Tone block with beater
 A second cassette tape recorder (optional)

Metal Sounds Accompaniment

The child creates an accompaniment to a recording.

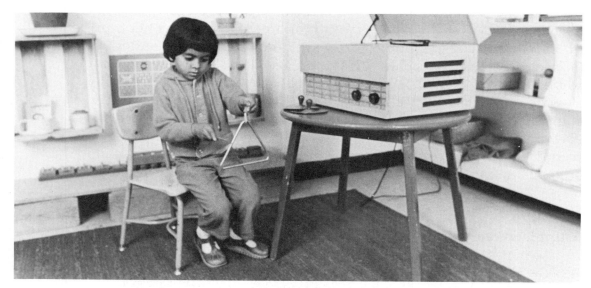

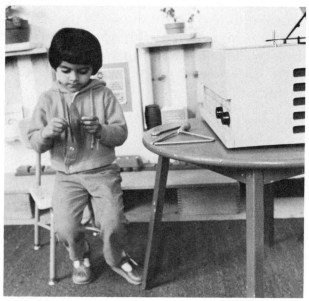

Activity

The child plays the triangle and cymbals to create an accompaniment to a recording.

Procedure

Invite the child to explore sound potentials of the triangle and cymbals. Help him or her learn to differentiate between metallic sounds and sounds made by other kinds of rhythm instruments (wood, skin, plastic, etc.).

Ask the child to listen to the recording "Drummer's March" and think how to use the triangle and cymbals to create a rhythmic accompaniment. Eventually the child plays along with the march, changing instruments at random, or at the end of the very obvious sections of music. Encourage him or her to make up interesting rhythms, but to play them at a loudness level appropriate for the recording. The child may wish to have several opportunities to play with the recording before giving a final performance for you, and perhaps other children.

*Supplementary Activity

Ask the child to identify some other instruments that produce metallic sounds (jingle clog, tambourine, jingle bells, finger cymbals, etc.). Tell the child to invite friends to play each of the available instruments; they all make up parts to accompany the recording. Remind them to play at a loudness level that will not overpower the recording.

Materials

Phonograph
Recording of "Drummer's March"
Triangle with beater
Cymbals

*Other metallic sound instruments such as tambourine, jingle bells, finger cymbals, jingle clogs

Drum Improvisation

The child improvises an accompaniment to recorded music. (See page xv for special instructions.)

Activity

The child uses two drums of different pitch to improvise an accompaniment to recorded piano music.

Procedure

Give the child the two drums. Permit him or her to freely play them for a few minutes and enjoy their sounds. Later ask the child to identify which drum has the higher pitch, and which has the lower pitch, and to demonstrate playing loud and soft on each of the drums. Next, invite the child to make up a drum piece for both drums that includes examples of loud and soft. Play the recording "Drummer's March" and ask him or her to make up a drum part to go with the recording, using both drums and loud and soft parts that correspond with the recorded piano music. You may want to tape record a performance of the recorded piano music and the child's drum improvisation to play back later for reflection and evaluation. Repeat this activity on another day.

*Supplementary Activity

Give the child rhythm sticks and invite him or her to make up another accompaniment for "Drummer's March." This activity could be extended further by having several children improvise accompanying parts using several different rhythm instruments.

Materials

Two small drums of different pitch (with beater)
Phonograph
Recording of "Drummer's March"
Cassette tape recorder

*Rhythm sticks

Broomstick Chime Improvisation

The child improvises tunes on a broomstick chime.

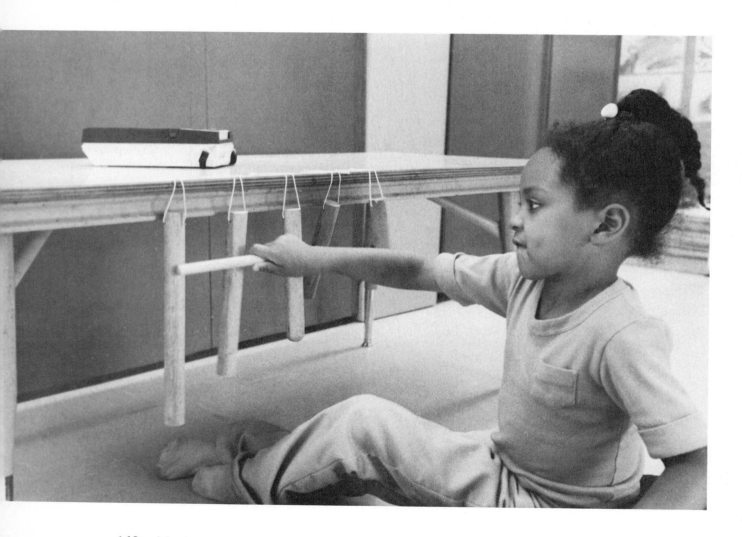

Activity

The child explores the sound potentials of a broomstick chime and then improvises tunes.

Procedure

Invite the child to play the broomstick chime and explore its sound potentials. Guide him or her to discover the pitch variations of the different stick pieces—the longer the stick the lower the pitch, the shorter the stick the higher the pitch. You also might help the child discover where to strike the different sticks to produce the most resonant and pleasing sounds. Eventually leave the child to work alone, making up tunes and trying out loud and soft, fast and slow, etc. Later return and ask the child to play some tunes for you. Record one of the improvisations to play back later.

*Supplementary Activity

Play the recording "Drum Rhythms." Ask the child to accompany it, by improvising a tune on the broomstick chime. Eventually make a tape recording of the performance for later listening and evaluation.

Materials

Broomstick chime (pieces of broomstick cut to different lengths and suspended from a frame by string; see picture)
Wooden dowel beater
Cassette tape recorder

*Phonograph
 Recording of "Drum Rhythms"

Chord Improvisations

The child improvises an accompaniment on two resonator bells.

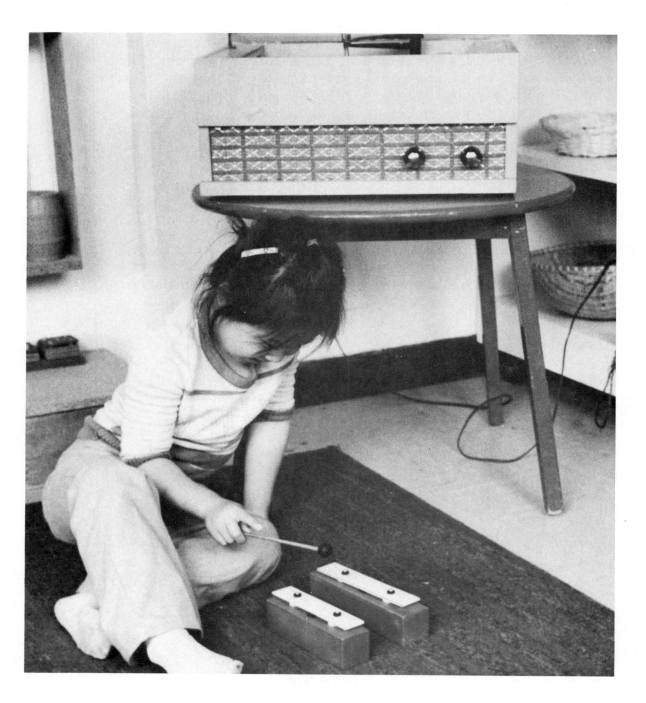

Activity

The child improvises an accompaniment on two resonator bells that corresponds with the chord changes heard in recorded music.

Procedure

Invite the child to play and enjoy the sounds of the C and F resonator bells, then make up something interesting to play for you later.

"Chord Improvisation Music" is organized so that the first eight beats utilize the C chord (C bell), and the next eight beats the F chord (F bell). The music then alternates between eight beats of C and eight beats of F. Play the recording for the child; help him or her learn to recognize the change of chords after each eight beats. Eventually guide the child to make up a part to play on the C bell each time the C chord sounds, and a part on the F bell each time the F chord sounds. Repeat this activity several times, especially on another day.

*Supplementary Activity

Give the child the two groups of bells (C, E, G for the C chord; F, A, C for the F chord). Arrange the bells so the groups are slightly separated. For this improvisation, the child plays any bells in the C chord group when the C chord sounds in "Chord Improvisation Music," and any bells in the F chord when the F chord sounds. You might help by pointing to the bell groups as the chords change in the music.

Materials

Phonograph
Recording of "Chord Improvisation Music"
Resonator bells C and F and playing mallet

*Resonator bells for Supplementary Activity (C, E, G; F, A, C)

School Sounds Composition

The children create a sound story of school activities.

Activity

The children identify certain sounds associated with their school life; they order selected sounds and record them to create a sound story.

Procedure

Have the children close their eyes, listen to, and identify all the sounds they can hear. Then ask them to name sounds they might hear during a school day (greeting, playground, equipment, toy, singing, food serving, clean-up, group activities, water, departure sounds, etc.). Have the children select and order sounds they feel best describe a typical school day. Record them. Some sounds could be produced by the children, others may need to be recorded in their natural setting at different times. Play the recording for the children and ask them to identify the sounds as higher-lower pitch, longer-shorter durations, and louder-softer. Later invite them to create a new sound story that includes interesting and contrasting sounds.

Supplementary Activity

Invite the children to use their voices and other sound sources to create a sound story that describes a familiar event: going to a park to play then returning home, having fun at the beach, enjoying rides at a carnival, going to a football game, playing tag, etc.

Materials

Cassette tape recorder
Equipment and other items necessary for producing selected sounds

Melody Improvisation

The child improvises a melody on resonator bells.

Activity

Using five resonator bells, the child improvises a melody that begins and ends on a tonic pitch.

Procedure

Invite the child to freely play the five resonator bells for a while. Help him or her understand that the size of the bell is related to its pitch—the larger the bell the lower the pitch, the smaller the bell the higher the pitch. Next, ask the child to make up a tune, including the sounds of all five bells, but beginning and ending with the sound of the largest (lowest pitched) bell. Point out that a tune beginning and ending on the lowest pitched bell sounds complete.

After a period of improvisation, tape record a performance. Play it back. If the child does not like it, he or she may want to make another to improve upon the first. Repeat this activity on another day.

*Supplementary Activity

Give the child a maraca. Play back the recorded bell performance and invite him or her to add a maraca improvisation. The child will enjoy hearing a recording of the combined bell and maraca improvisations (use a second cassette tape recorder). Be certain to play back the recording for the child to enjoy and evaluate.

Materials

Resonator bells C, D, E, G, A with beater
Cassette tape recorder

*Maraca
 A second cassette tape recorder (optional)

Improvising Rhythms

The child improvises an accompaniment for a recorded piano selection.

Activity

The child selects a rhythm instrument to play and makes up a part to accompany a recorded piano selection.

Procedure

Invite the child to select an instrument(s) to play and to take some time to produce sounds with it. Ask him or her to listen to "Blues Music" and to begin playing along with the recording. Encourage the child to make up interesting parts but to try to play in time with the beat and at a loudness level appropriate for the piano sounds. Repeat several times.

Supplementary Activity

After several children have participated in the activity, invite them to play different instruments to accompany the song. They should attempt to play in time with the beat, keeping their combined sound at a loudness level appropriate for the level of the recording.

Materials

Rhythm instruments (jingle clog, tone block, maracas, finger cymbals, or notched gourd)
Phonograph
Recording of "Blues Music"

Tambourine Sounds

The child uses a tambourine and other items in creative ways to produce a variety of sounds.

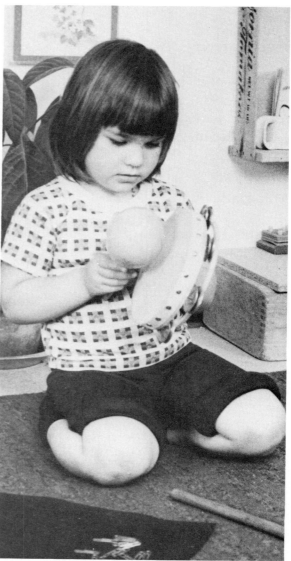

Activity

The child experiments and discovers a variety of ways to produce sounds of different durations and timbres using a tambourine and selected objects.

Procedure

Give the child a tambourine and ask him or her to play it in a variety of ways, making as many different sounds as possible of varying durations and timbres. Eventually give the child an assortment of items to use to produce an even wider variety of sounds. Prompt his or her discovery only when necessary. Sounds may be produced by shaking, rubbing, tapping, striking the tambourine. Striking the skin of the instrument with a stick, a maraca, a tennis ball, different parts of the body, etc., will produce a variety of sounds. Placing items such as paper clips, dried peas, alphabet blocks, sand, tinker toys, buttons inside the tambourine then shaking the instrument also will produce a variety of sounds. Later, have the child share with you all the different sounds discovered.

*Supplementary Activity

Play the recording "Music for Tambourine" and ask the child to listen. The second time, invite him or her to make up a part on the tambourine to accompany the music, using some of the interesting sounds discovered.

Materials

Tambourine
Assorted items such as rhythm sticks, maracas, tennis balls, buttons, dried peas, alphabet blocks, tinker toys, sand, pebbles

*Phonograph
 Recording of "Music for Tambourine"

Composition for Resonator Bells

The child creates and notates a composition for resonator bells.

Activity

The child composes a piece for three resonator bells using line notation, then rehearses and performs it.

Procedure

Give the child the three resonator bells. After a period of exploration, ask which bells have the highest, lowest, and middle pitches. When the child can recognize the pitches as high, middle, and low, have him or her line them up in order with the lowest bell on the left, the highest on the right. Draw three short lines on a sheet of paper

and ask the child to show you the highest, lowest, and middle line, then play this notation. When he or she can associate the height of the line with the pitches of the bells, draw another pattern such as and ask him or her to practice playing it.

Eventually give the child a sheet of paper to compose a piece consisting of high, middle, and low resonator bell pitches. He or she should practice playing it and be prepared to play it for you later. Invite the child to compose another piece for three bells on another day.

*Supplementary Activity

Give children who are ready to extend the activity five bells to line up in order from lowest to highest. They then compose a piece using line notation.

Materials

Three resonator bells

C E G

Resonator bell mallet
Several sheets of paper
Felt-tip pen

*Two additional resonator bells for *Supplementary Activity*

D A

Jar Melodies

The child improvises melodic patterns to accompany recorded rhythms.

Activity

The child improvises melodic patterns using jars filled with water to accompany recorded rhythms played on a drum set.

Procedure

Play the recording "Drum Rhythms" and invite the child to listen and move to the music. Ask him or her to listen to it a second time and try to decide how many sections are in the music, and what makes them sound different. Help the child discover that there is a brief pause at the end of each section, and that each section sounds different because a different combination of sounds is heard.

Give the child the three jars and the wooden beater with which to experiment and then make up a melody. Later invite him or her to improvise a melody while listening to the recorded drum set rhythms. The improvisation should be—as much as possible—played in time with the beat of the recorded music. Repeat this activity on other days.

*Supplementary Activity

With the five resonator bells and beater, the child makes up another melody to play with the drum set rhythms. You might record the performance and the recorded drum set sounds for later listening and evaluation.

Materials

Phonograph
Recording of "Drum Rhythms"
Three jars filled to different levels with water (three different pitches)
Wooden tone block beater

*Resonator bells:

Resonator bell beater
Cassette tape recorder

Kazoo Improvisations

The child improvises tunes on a kazoo.

Activity

The child improvises tunes on a kazoo to recorded accompaniment music.

Procedure

Ask the child to hum the tune of a familiar song with you. When you are confident the child knows how to hum, ask him or her to hum and make up a tune. Eventually demonstrate where to place the mouth on a kazoo, and invite the child to hum into the instrument. Guide him or her to eventually play a familiar tune on the kazoo. With some proficiency on the instrument, the child can play along with the recording "Drum Rhythms," making up tunes. Repeat this activity on other days.

*Supplementary Activity

Play the recording of "Drum Rhythms" again, and invite three or more children to play together, making up tunes on their kazoos. Guide them to add other instruments (such as rhythm sticks, finger cymbals, jingle clogs).

Materials

Phonograph
Recording of "Drum Rhythms"
Kazoos

*Rhythm sticks, finger cymbals, jingle clogs

Accompaniment Improvisation

The child improvises an accompaniment on an autoharp.

Activity

The child improvises parts on the autoharp to accompany a tape recording of a song.

Procedure

Place the autoharp on the floor or a table, and give the child a felt or plastic pick to strum the strings. After exploration time, show how to hold down the different chord buttons while strumming. Again permit him or her to play and explore the new way to produce different sounds. Now ask the child to hold down the F chord button (another child may hold it down) and strum the strings. Encourage short strums (striking only a few strings) and long strums (striking all the strings). Eventually play the cassette tape recording of "Are You Sleeping?" and ask the child to strum the F chord, making up an interesting part to accompany the song. Play the tape several times, encouraging different accompaniments to the singing. He or she might even experiment using different kinds of picks. Repeat this activity on another day.

*Supplementary Activity

Invite the child to again hold down the F chord button and improvise an accompaniment for the recording of "Are You Sleeping?" For these improvisations, several other children can improvise parts on rhythm instruments and join the performance. Permit the ensemble to improvise parts for several playings of the tape.

Materials

Autoharp with different kinds of picks
Cassette tape recorder
Cassette tape recording of someone singing "Are You Sleeping?" beginning on the pitch F

*Assorted rhythm instruments

Activities
Including
Two or More Arts

Mask Characters

The children create mask characters and improvise dialog.

Activity

The children add features to a basic mask form to create mask characters; they role-play their characters and improvise dialog.

Procedure

Demonstrate procedures involved in creating a mask character. You might have one volunteer wear a basic mask form as you add features to create a character.

When the children are ready, have the first two put on the basic form, then place cutout features on each other. When completed, they should take a good look at themselves in a mirror to find out what they look like. They then improvise dialog and walk as they feel their mask characters should. If a child's mask has a scar, the dialog could include an explanation about the accident that caused the scar. Dialog can explain why another mask has funny-looking hair. Encourage the children to create interesting movements for their characters. After they have time to develop characters, they should remove the cutout features from the mask forms and return them to the box for the next pair to use.

*Supplementary Activity

Provide the children with assorted materials and invite them to create their own cutout features for the mask forms. They then engage in improvised dialog with each other, or individually give a short improvised scene that tells about the character developed.

Materials

Two basic mask forms made from two rectangular pieces (approximately 12″ x 20″) of material that include cut-out holes to allow for eyes, mouth, and nose
Scraps of fabric, felt, and other materials cut into a variety of shapes for eyes, eyebrows, teeth, tongues, eye patches, hair, hairline shapes, glasses, scars, etc. (each cutout includes a backing of two-way tape)
Scissors
Two-way tape

*Scraps of assorted materials

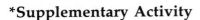

"Pop" Shapes

The children move creatively in response to musical cues.

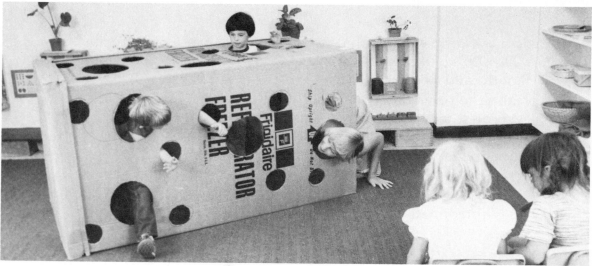

Activity

The children go inside a box; they listen to recorded music and use their body parts in creative ways to protrude through holes in the box at times suggested by the music.

Procedure

Invite two or three children at a time to go inside the box with you and explore the space. Encourage them to experiment putting their heads through the larger holes, arms and legs through the smaller holes. Make certain each child has an opportunity to explore and enjoy the box.

Play the recording "Pop Goes the Mouse." Some children may immediately clap their hands or make other sounds when they hear the "pop." When all are familiar with the music, ask two children at a time to go inside the box. They listen to the music, then stick out their heads, arms, and/or legs at the pop points in the music. They should use the holes in the box and their body parts as creatively as possible. A unique facial expression in combination with an arm or leg will result in interesting shapes and immediate enjoyment for the children. Give each child an opportunity to use the holes in the box for a creative display.

*Supplementary Activity

Give each child a rhythm instrument. Play the recording again and ask the children to play their instruments at the "pops" in the music. A second time, ask the children to move about the room in some interesting way in time with the beat. They are to use their imaginations and play their instruments in some unique way (between legs, behind the back, up high, down low, etc.) at the pops. Encourage originality and creative uses of the instruments and bodies.

Materials

Refrigerator or other appliance box with head, arm, leg size holes cut
   out at random
Phonograph
Recording of "Pop Goes the Mouse"

*Rhythm instruments (one for each child)

Moving and Freezing

The children move creatively and freeze in response to recorded music.

Activity

The children move creatively in a variety of ways to different sections of music; they freeze in interesting positions when the music stops.

Procedure

Ask the children to imitate your movements. For instance, swing your arms and body for about fifteen seconds, then freeze in an interesting position. As the children imitate your actions, include a variety of movements such as walking, running, leaping, jumping, hopping, skipping, sliding, shimmering, swaying, twisting, turning, bending, stretching, jerking, and spinning.

When the children understand the procedure, tell them they will again move and freeze, this time without your lead, to the recording "Moving and Freezing Music." Each section suggests different kinds of movement. Encourage the children to move as they want, then to freeze in an interesting position and remain stationary until the music begins again.

*Supplementary Activity

Give each child a rhythm instrument and play the recording "Moving and Freezing Music." This time the children are to move and play their instruments when they hear music, freeze in a position and keep their instruments silent when the music stops. Encourage originality in this combination of moving and playing.

Materials

Phonograph
Recording of "Moving and Freezing Music"
Assorted rhythm instruments

*Assorted rhythm instruments

Slow Motion Ball

The children pantomime playing with a ball in slow motion.

Activity

The children pantomime playing with a ball in a variety of ways, creating interesting movements in slow motion.

Procedure

Demonstrate how to play with a large ball in a variety of ways. You might walk across the room bouncing it like a basketball, or roll, kick, throw, toss, catch, twirl it. Ask the children to either identify or show other ways to play with a ball.

Have the children imagine they each have a ball. They are to pantomime doing different things with their balls in slow motion. You may need to demonstrate slow motion movements. At first they may only imitate you; eventually encourage them to make up their own slow motion movements.

Supplementary Activity

Suggest that the children play a game of tag in slow motion. Encourage concentration on moving slowly and creating unique movements for tagging and running away.

Materials

Large rubber or plastic ball that will bounce

Scarf Creations

The children use scarves in creative ways in response to recorded music.

Activity

The children move in response to recorded music, using scarves in creative ways to represent the contrasting sections they hear.

Procedure

Give the children scarves to experiment with (shake it, wave it slowly, toss it up and let it fall, move it in a circular motion above the head, make a figure eight, etc.). Next, play the recording "Waltz-Tremolo." Ask them to listen and move their scarves in ways that look like the music sounds. The two alternating sections are clearly different and suggestive of contrasting uses of the scarves. Encourage the children to use them differently each time they hear a waltz section, and each time they hear a tremolo section. They will probably, in a natural response, move their bodies while moving the scarves.

Supplementary Activity

Ask the children to experiment using the scarves to represent water in various forms (ocean waves, rain, waterfall, fountain, rain storm, the downstream rushing of a river, garden spray, etc.). Encourage them to make up a story to tell while depicting water with scarves.

Materials

Lightweight scarves, approximately 36″ long and 10″ wide
Phonograph
Recording of "Waltz-Tremolo"

Notating Familiar Sounds

The child creates graphic notation to represent sounds.

Activity

The child identifies ten familiar sounds, vocally imitates the sounds, and creates graphic notation to represent them.

Procedure

Invite the child to name a familiar sound such as wind blowing, ambulance siren, rain drops, car motor, cat meows, brushing of teeth, then vocally imitate it. He or she then should draw a simple picture to represent the sound, using imagination. A wind sound might look something like ᴕ ᴕ ᴕ , rain drops ∴∴∴, brushing of teeth ∿∿∿. Help the child create pictures (notation) to approximate the general pitch direction (high, low), and duration (long, short) aspects of the sounds. The child can then perform from the pictures, imitating the sounds the pictures represent.

Supplementary Activity

Extend the activity by having the child collect toys that make different sounds, then create pictures (notation) that look like those sounds.

Materials

Paper
Felt-tip pen

Talking Faces

The children create faces and tell stories about them.

Activity

The children are given felt-tip pens and sheets of paper with the outline of a head. They create faces by drawing in features, then tell stories about the faces.

Procedure

Give the children felt-tip pens and sheets of paper with the outline of a head. Invite them to create faces by drawing in features. You may need to guide, reminding them to include features such as eyes, ears, nose, mouth, eyebrows. For some features they may want to use a different size felt-tip pen. They can add lines to their faces, include hair, and even objects in the hair where appropriate. Encourage them to make their faces interesting. When they finish, have them take turns telling brief stories about the faces.

Supplementary Activity

Invite the children (by pairs) to create dialogs between their faces—they face each other and hold their paper faces in front of them. They create a dialog from a subject they choose or suggested subjects, such as "What do you like to eat?" "Why are you smiling (frowning)?" "What are your favorite games?" "What do you like to do when you go home from school?" "What television programs do you like and why?" "Why does your hair look like that?"

Materials

8½" x 11" sheets with the outline of a head (see Master No. 5 in *Appendix*)
Assorted sizes of felt-tip pens

Butterfly Process

The children move creatively to pantomime a metamorphosis.

Activity

The children move creatively in response to recorded music to pantomime a caterpillar becoming a butterfly.

Procedure

Arrange to have in your classroom a caterpillar or butterfly eggs on a leaf so the children may observe the metamorphosis process. After they have observed the entire change, involve them in a brief discussion about what they have seen. Help them recall the different events: eggs hatching, caterpillar worms eating, growing bigger, spinning of the cocoon, waiting to be free, and finally emerging as a butterfly.

Play the recording "Butterfly Music" and help the children recognize where the music suggests the different hatching events. When they are familiar with the music, invite them to listen again and act out the events. You may need to do some side coaching to guide the children and encourage originality. We recommend you repeat the movement part of this activity on another day.

Supplementary Activity

Have the children help you create a brief story to be read during the stages of the hatching. Mention wind, rain, sunshine, or other things that might affect the caterpillar, the cocoon, or the butterfly. Some children could play act the weather, as the others pantomime the change.

Materials

Bottle with caterpillar
Phonograph
Recording of "Butterfly Music"

Balloon Dance

The children move creatively with a balloon in response to recorded music.

Activity

The children move creatively with a balloon in response to brief contrasting sections of recorded music.

Procedure

Have the children sit in a circle around the balloon. Play the recording "Balloon Dance," and tell the children as they listen to the music they will take turns going to the center and doing something unique with their bodies and the balloon. For instance, the first section is a march. A child might decide to march to the music while bouncing the balloon. A child may lie on the floor and move the balloon with his feet for the fourth section (slow blues). For the fifth, a gallop, a child might run in a gallop while moving the balloon over his or her head in a circular pattern.

There are only six contrasting sections, so begin the recording again after the sixth child has moved to the jazz section. Encourage the children to be imaginative.

Supplementary Activity

Play the recording again, and invite four children to move in the center of the circle to all six sections of the music. They must relate with their bodies, moving their balloons, to each other (such as hitting their balloons together for the march section, tossing their balloons to each other—high in the air—for the floating section, tapping a rhythm on each other's balloons for the jazz section).

Materials

Phonograph
Recording of "Balloon Dance"
Weather balloons (may be purchased from the Weather Bureau in your
   area) or other types of large, strong balloons, partially inflated

Paper Sack Puppets

The children create puppets and improvise dialog.

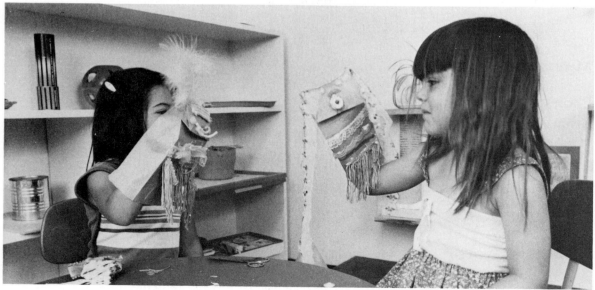

Activity

The children use paper sacks to create puppets; they select partners and improvise dialog between their puppets.

Procedure

Demonstrate how to make a paper sack puppet. Use it to talk with the children, eventually inviting them to make their own puppets.

When the children complete their puppets, have them select partners. The partners use their puppets to engage in improvised pleasant conversation. They may talk about favorite foods, toys, T.V. programs, stories, play activities, etc. Use your puppet to stimulate conversation between the partner puppets.

*Supplementary Activity

Invite the children to create a collection of monster puppets of different sizes. They may wish to make their puppets hairy (use yarn, newspaper, cloth scraps, etc.) and include grotesque facial features. Encourage them to make their monster puppets as interesting as possible. Later have them improvise dialog suitable for puppet monsters, using monster voice tones.

Materials

Small paper sacks (one for each child)
Construction paper
Scissors
Glue with brushes

*Several larger paper sacks of different sizes

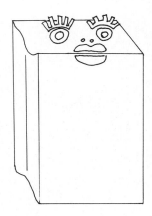

Body Part Improvisations

The children move creatively in response to recorded rhythms.

Activity

The children use different body parts to move creatively to recorded rhythms played on a drum set.

Procedure

Invite the children to listen to the recording "Drum Rhythms" and move to the music. Help them discover the four sections in the music. Each section is concluded by a brief pause; each sounds different because of the different combination of instruments. When they recognize the four sections, ask them to create movements using different body parts. For the first section, they use only hands; second section, arms; third section, feet (standing or sitting); fourth section, entire body. Encourage them to do interesting things with their body parts as they move, and try not to look like the other children.

Supplementary Activity

Extend the activity, using the same recording, by asking children to create interesting movements using other body parts such as fingers, heads, shoulders, hips.

Materials

Phonograph
Recording of "Drum Rhythms"

Dance: *Movement, Time*
Music: *Timbre*

Nuts, Bolts, and Springs

The children move creatively in response to sounds they hear in a recording.

186   *Two or More Arts*

Activity

The children create machine-like movements, which they repeat in response to different sounds in recorded music.

Procedure

Invite the children to demonstrate with their body parts interesting, machine-like movements. Have children moving in some unique way share their movements with the others. Eventually ask the children to listen to the recording "Nuts, Bolts, and Springs Music." Help them learn to recognize the five different sounds that are added one by one until all are sound simultaneously, then gradually exit until the last sound ends.

Select five children to create interesting movements to the five sounds. Play the recording again. Each child moves only as long as his or her sound is heard, otherwise remaining frozen. Give all the children in the group an opportunity to move in response to the recorded sounds.

Supplementary Activity

Select a theme such as candy makers or bubble gum makers and invite the children to create new movements for the recording "Nuts, Bolts, and Springs Music." The children stand in line, moving from left to right in response to their assigned sounds. By repeating their movements, they develop the idea of an assembly line.

Materials

Phonograph
Recording of "Nuts, Bolts, and Springs Music"

Body Part Designs

The children move creatively to draw shapes with body parts. (See page xv for special instructions.)

Activity

The children use their body parts creatively to draw in the air a variety of geometric shapes and lines.

Procedure

Give the children drawing paper and pencils, and help them learn to draw (approximate) circles, squares, and triangles. When they can distinguish among the three shapes, ask them, looking at their circles, to draw circles in the air with one hand. Similarly, help them draw squares and triangles in the air.

   When the children can draw all three shapes in the air on your signal, invite them to draw the shapes, one by one, using different body parts. For instance, they might draw a circle with a shoulder, elbow, seat, leg, knee, foot, toe, head, chest. Make certain all the children share some unique way they have used body parts. You may eventually want to add other geometric figures or lines such as ∿, ⋎⋎⋎⋎⋎, and ⟋⟍. Encourage the children to share lines or figures they think of drawing.

*Supplementary Activity

Play the recording of "Slow Jazz Patterns" and permit the children to move freely to the music. Then suggest they do a dance, drawing a square for four beats with a hand, four beats with a knee, four beats with the chest, four beats with a foot. The music is 32 measures long (four beats to a measure), which means they can do the whole sequence eight times. They may later create a dance using several geometric figures or lines, or making up their own plan.

Materials

Drawing paper
Pencils

*Phonograph
 Recording of "Slow Jazz Patterns"

Clam Chatter

The children create clams and improvise dialogs.

Activity

The children create clams from paper plates and make their clams talk as they improvise dialogs.

Procedure

Have the children make clams: first they fold one plate in half, then cut the plate into two equal halves (cut on the fold indentation). Now they fold the second plate in a similar manner (do not cut it into halves). They glue the curved edges of the two halves onto the folded plate. The straight edge of each plate half should be left unglued so the children can slip four fingers into the top half, and the thumb into the lower half.

   Let the children have a few minutes to learn to operate their clams. Then suggest they add features such as teeth, eyes, nose, hair, line designs. They may wish to work with only a black felt-tip pen, or with paints and crayons. Ask questions as they work to stimulate creative thought. When their clams are completed, invite the children (by twos) to operate their clams and engage in dialog. They may discuss why the clams look like they do, or create dialogs on a variety of subjects. Encourage all the children to get their clams to "talk" with the other clams. Occasionally have them switch partners, and sometimes talk in groups of three.

*Supplementary Activity

Invite the children to create a variety of interesting clams with assorted sizes of paper plates. They might make monster clams, people clams, robot clams, clown clams. Eventually they operate their menagerie of clams and improvise a story. You will need to operate one clam and develop a theme to involve all the other clams in the story.

Materials

Two plain paper plates for each child (5″ to 7″ in diameter)
Scissors
Glue with brushes
Crayons
Paints
Felt-tip pens

*Assorted sizes of paper plates

Mechanical Toys

The children move creatively as mechanical toys in a contained space.

Activity

The children pantomime mechanical toys and move creatively to change direction as they bump into imaginary walls.

Procedure

With a shallow box and a small metal ball, show the children how a ball will change direction when it bumps into a wall or another obstacle within a contained space. Mark off a circle on the floor; tell them to imagine an invisible wall where they see the tape. You might first walk into the invisible wall, bounce off and go in another direction until you bump into another invisible wall, and so on. Help them expand their understanding of direction (backward, sideward, forward) as you bump into invisible walls.

Next, pantomime a mechanical toy that, after being wound up, walks very stiffly and takes short steps. As your toy bumps into the circle walls, it changes direction. Gradually involve the children in pantomiming mechanical toys that bump into the walls and each other and change direction. Include only a few children in the circle at a time to prevent too many collisions. Encourage the toys to use their imaginations.

Supplementary Activity

You may extend the activity by having children assume different toy roles (hobby horse, teddy bear, monster toy, drummer boy, robot, etc.) and move in unqiue ways to bump into invisible walls and change direction.

Materials

Masking tape to mark off a circle on the floor, approximately 15' in diameter
Metal ball and small box

Creating and Dramatizing a Story

The children create a story and dramatize it using movement and sound.

Activity

The children create and dramatize a story using movement, props, and sound to describe the different events.

Procedure

Invite the children to help you create a brief story describing an event of interest to them (trip to the zoo, walking tour around the block, shopping for a toy, etc.). Read the completed story to the children several times and ask them to tell or show how the different events could be dramatized. Help them decide what actions to use in their dramatizations. Ask what sounds might describe the events in the story (for instance: walking—woodblock sounds; wind—shaking tambourine sounds; siren—voice sounds; car motor—recorded fan motor or other motor sounds; animal—voice sounds). Assign parts, rehearse the various events, then have them perform as you read the story.

Supplementary Activity

Invite the children to create another story to dramatize. After several groups in the school have created stories and learned to dramatize them, have the groups perform their stories for each other.

Materials

Items for events in the story

Music for Moving

The children move creatively in response to music.

Activity

The children listen to contrasting sections of music and create a variety of movements in response to what they hear.

Procedure

Ask children to listen to the recording "Contrasting Sections" and move in response to the music. When they are familiar with the music, invite them to play a game—they will create unique movements for the different sections.

Mark off a triangular area, with the three triangle points approximately 20' apart. Use chairs or other furniture to identify the three points. The children take turns going on a journey along the triangular path. As they hear the first section of music, they move from the first point to the second with a unique movement. For the second section, they move with a different movement between the second and third points, and so on from third back to the original point. Eventually the game may be played with three children moving simultaneously, each departing from different points. Encourage them to create unique movements to the sounds of the music.

Supplementary Activity

Extend the activity by having all the children form a circle. They move clockwise (in a circle) to the first section of music, counterclockwise to the second, clockwise to the third, etc. The children take turns as leader, and all children must move as the leader moves—in some unique way to each section of the music.

Materials

Phonograph
Recording of "Contrasting Sections"

Sound and Movement Story

The child places pictures in a desired order to create a story, then acts it out using movements and sounds.

Activity

The child creates a story by placing pictures of activities in a desired order, then acts it out using movements and sounds to illustrate the activities.

Procedure

Show the child the pictures you have collected, and ask him or her to role-play the activity in each picture. Show them one at a time again and ask the child to use voice (or other sound source) to describe the pictured activity in sound. Eventually the child should be able to role-play and produce sounds for each activity.

Invite the child to create a story by placing the pictures in a desired order. It could begin with sleeping, then waking up, preparing for school, going to school, etc.; or begin in school, then running or walking home, eating, preparing to go to bed, sleeping, etc. Guide the child to determine the order of the different events in the story. After placing the pictures in a desired order, he or she acts out the story by using contrasting movements and sounds to illustrate each activity pictured.

*Supplementary Activity

Give the child the other set of pictures (such as bouncing a ball, riding a hobby horse, playing jump-rope, washing dishes, sweeping floor, riding a bus, raking leaves, playing with a toy) with which to create another story. He or she should first line up the pictures in a desired order, then use movements and sounds to illustrate the activities.

Materials

Simple line drawings or pictures of different activities from a coloring book (a child sleeping, waking up, washing face, eating, brushing teeth, walking, running, in school, talking with other children, putting on clothes, etc.)

*A different set of pictures describing assorted activities familiar to the child

Finger Puppets

The children create finger puppets, assume roles, and improvise dialog.

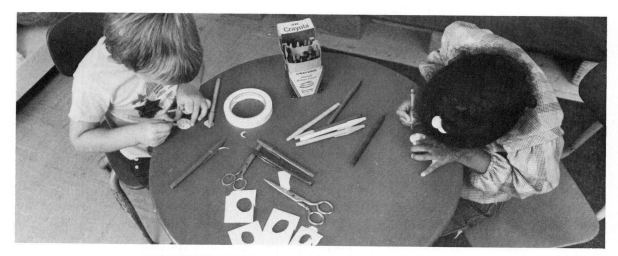

Activity

With felt-tip pens, the children create faces (human, animal, monster, etc.) on oval-shaped pieces of paper. They attach the faces to their fingers and improvise dialog in pairs.

Procedure

Invite the children to practice drawing faces on the oval pieces of paper with felt-tip pens. Suggest they experiment using different kinds of lines (heavy, light) and giving the faces different expressions (happy, sad). They attach the completed faces to their index fingers with two-way tape. As their finger puppets then face each other, they are ready for dialog.

Encourage the children to make up a dialog between their finger puppets, about something of interest such as a trip to the zoo, a favorite game, good foods, favorite stories, fun things to do, best toys. Should the children have difficulty assuming roles for the faces, you might prepare your own finger puppet and initiate dialog between your puppet and one of theirs.

*Supplementary Activity

After several children have created finger puppets, invite them to have their puppets talk with each other. The children may want to make clothes for their puppets from paper and/or cloth scraps.

Materials

Precut oval-shaped pieces of paper
Felt-tip pens
Two-way tape

*Scraps of paper and/or cloth

Kitchen Utensil Shapes

The children create representational movements in response to recorded music.

Activity

The children listen to recorded music and move in creative ways to represent various kitchen utensils.

Procedure

Show the children the different kitchen utensils. Invite them to do something with their bodies to look like one of the utensils. As you point to each child, have the others guess what utensil the child looks like. Make certain the children represent all five utensils. Eventually have them show you what their utensils would look like marching around the room.

Play the first five sections of the recording "Utensil March." Ask the children which sections they would like to have represent the different utensils. Play the recording again. Those representing the utensil for the first section march in a circle as they hear the music, then those representing the second section, and so on. On the sixth section all utensils join in the parade for a final march.

Supplementary Activity

Assemble some of the larger toys in one area of the room. Ask the children to do something with their bodies to represent one of the toys. You might play "Utensil March" again and invite the toys to parade around the room.

Materials

Utensils (fork, cup, saucer, pan, little spoon)
Phonograph
Recording of "Utensil March"

Frog's Feast (A Sound Story)

The children plan for and present a creative performance of a sound story.

Activity

The children originate ways to dramatize actions in a story and select sound sources to highlight actions; they creatively perform a sound story.

Procedure

Read the story "Frog's Feast" to the children. (You may want to modify or abbreviate the story for the children in your group.) Discuss the different events, then read it again, this time asking the children to think in terms of sound effects that might be used in the story. Here are suggested sound effect cues (S.E.) and sound sources:

Hop sounds: papa frog—low-pitched tone block
               mama frog—medium-pitched tone block
               baby frog—high-pitched tone block

Ribitch sounds: papa frog—low-pitched notched instrument
                such as guiro
                mama frog—medium-pitched notched instrument
                baby frog—high-pitched notched instrument

Rubbing sound: sandpaper blocks

Buzzing sounds: mouth sounds

Tongue-catching mosquito sounds: hit two sticks together

Swallowing sounds: mouth sounds

Swatting sounds: hit two sandpaper blocks together

Help the children choose the actions in the story they will dramatize, and the sound sources they will use for effects.

Supplementary Activity

Select a story familiar to the children and suggest that they think of ways to pantomime actions and use sound sources to reinforce actions. As they try out their ideas, guide them to make the final selection of actions and sounds. A performance of the story could be shared with other groups of children in the school.

Materials

Assorted rhythm instruments as suggested in *Procedure* above, and those suggested by children in your group

Frog's Feast (A Sound Story)

In a little pond full of water lilies, a family of frogs lived—a papa frog, a mama frog, and a baby frog. Everyday they would hop from lily pad to lily pad looking for a delicious mosquito to eat (S.E.—three different-pitched tone blocks sounding together). One day the papa frog jumped out of the water onto a lily pad (S.E.), and looked all around to see if the area was safe. When he saw it was, he croaked to the mama frog to join him. She jumped onto a lily pad next to the papa frog (S.E.). She too looked around to check for danger before calling the baby frog. When she saw there was no threat of danger she called in her sweet croak for her baby frog (S.E.). Then they sang like frogs do in the summer when the sun slowly disappears and the sky darkens (S.E.).

The papa frog began to rub his stomach (S.E.) and think how nice it would be to catch a fat, juicy mosquito for dinner. All at once he heard a buzzing sound (S.E.). He sat very still and followed the flying mosquito with his eyes (S.E.). When the mosquito flew close to his mouth, he snapped out his long tongue, caught it (S.E.), and quickly swallowed it (S.E.). Then another mosquito buzzed by (S.E.), and once again the papa frog caught it and swallowed it (S.E.). After eating two juicy mosquitos he jumped into the pond and swam away.

The mama frog also wanted dinner before going to sleep, so she too sat very still and waited for a mosquito. Soon she heard a buzzing sound as another mosquito flew by (S.E.). When the mosquito flew close to her mouth she stuck out her long tongue, caught the mosquito, and swallowed it with a quick gulp (S.E.). Feeling content with her meal, she jumped into the pond and swam away.

Now the baby frog—who had been busy all this time making faces at his reflection in the water—realized how hungry he was. So he decided to catch himself a fat mosquito to eat. Far away he could hear the buzzing sound of a mosquito. He sat very still and waited. Finally a mosquito appeared and buzzed around him (S.E.). The baby frog was a good student and practiced what his parents taught him. When the mosquito came close, he quickly stuck out his tongue (S.E.), but missed! The mosquito was too fast for him. The baby frog said to himself "I'll try again." Once more he snapped his tongue at another mosquito flying by (S.E.) and missed. Then he had a great idea. He decided to get into the water and hide among the lily pads; when a mosquito came to rest on a pad, he would jump up and swat it with his web foot. So he dove into the water and waited. Soon a mosquito came buzzing by (S.E.) and landed on a lily pad near the baby frog. Keeping his eyes on the mosquito, the baby frog slowly raised his leg, took aim, and swatted the mosquito with all his might (S.E.)! Then he lifted his foot to see the smashed mosquito. There was no mosquito—he had missed again. But this baby frog would not give up. He got another idea. This time he decided to hide under a lily pad, and when a mosquito landed on it, he would quickly turn it over and gulp down his dinner. He went under the water and waited beneath the pad. Suddenly, he heard a very loud buzzing sound (S.E.). "A real big one," he laughed to himself. He did not know that a big bumblebee had landed on the pad. The baby frog flipped over the lily pad and tried to gulp down the bumblebee (S.E.). He had some difficulty, but he managed to swallow what he thought was a great big mosquito. The baby frog smiled, feeling very proud of himself, until he began to hear a buzzing sound in his stomach (S.E.). The bumblebee was causing the baby frog's whole body to shake (S.E.). Then the baby frog swatted his stomach with his web foot (S.E.), and the buzzing stopped. He smiled, then swam away to look for his parents. But every so often he would again hear a buzzing sound coming from his stomach (S.E.), and he would again have to swat his stomach to stop the buzzing. The baby frog began to wonder if his stomach would keep buzzing for the rest of his life.

Space Adventure (A Sound Story)

The children plan and present a creative performance of a sound story.

Activity

The children choose creative ways to dramatize actions and use sound sources to highlight events in a story; they rehearse the story and later perform it for other children.

Procedure

Read the story to the children. (You may want to modify or abbreviate the story for the children in your group.) Later ask them to tell you what the story was about. Particularly help them to recall the sequence of events and identify the principal actions. Then the children plan a performance of the story that includes sound effects for selected events and dramatizations of actions. The sound effect points indicated in the story by S.E. are only suggested; these may be omitted and others substituted or added.

Encourage the children to explore a variety of ways to dramatize the events before deciding upon a set to use in performance. Also guide them to experiment with different sound sources to highlight actions. Solicit their suggestions, try out their ideas, and help them make decisions relative to the performance. After rehearsing the story, present a performance of it for other groups in the school.

Supplementary Activity

Invite the children to help you create another space adventure story about a space creature that has one arm, one leg, one eye, four ears, and no nose or mouth. Write the sequence of events suggested by the children, and then put them into story form. Rehearse and perform it on different days, permitting all the children to assume the various roles.

Materials

Assorted rhythm instruments and other sound sources

Space Adventure (A Sound Story)

In a little spaceship named Kupcak, Captain Mary and her robot dog Torbik were travelling through space (S.E.). They had been in outer space for many months exploring different planets. As they approached Earth, Captain Mary smiled, realizing she would soon be home. She began pushing the many different-colored buttons to steer the ship back to Earth. "Captain Mary," a voice spoke through the control panel. "Captain Mary here," she replied. "This is mission control; you are to go back into outer space and explore Asteroid B12." "But," replied Captain Mary, "we have been travelling for many months, and . . ." "Sorry, Captain Mary, you must follow orders," said the voice from the panel. "All right," the Captain answered in a disappointed voice, "roger, over and out."

Captain Mary called her robot dog, and Torbik came to her side wagging his mechanical tail (S.E.). The Captain strapped Torbik into his seat (S.E.) in preparation for the blastoff to Asteroid B12. The countdown began: 10, 9, 8, 7 . . . (S.E.). The spaceship's engines gave a sudden blast of sound (S.E.) and Captain Mary and Torbik could feel they were again heading out into space at a terrific speed. After awhile they began to slow down, then heard a loud thump (S.E.) as the Captain landed the ship on Asteroid B12. Captain Mary unfastened her and Torbik's seat belts (S.E.), got up, and began screwing on her space helmet (S.E.). She put her laser gun in its holster, pressed the red button to open the spaceship door (S.E.), and off they went to explore Asteroid B12.

They soon discovered that Asteroid B12 was a lonely place; no plants or animals lived there. All they could see were little dirt hills everywhere, and they heard a soft, mysterious wind blowing (S.E.). Suddenly Torbik began to sniff (S.E.) and growl (S.E.), pointing his nose at one little dirt hill. Captain Mary ran to the spot (S.E.), brushed the dirt away (S.E.), and, surprised, saw a tiny door with a little door knob. The Captain turned the door knob but the door was tight and would not move. She tried again, using all her strength. Finally, it began to open with a weird squeaking sound (S.E.). There, much to her amazement, were steps leading down to a long passageway. "Hello," Captain Mary called out. But all she heard was her own echo (S.E.). Since there was no answer, she and her robot dog went down the stairs (S.E.) and their footsteps echoed as they walked through the passageway (S.E.). The Captain saw a bright light at the end of the passageway; when she reached the light she looked, and her mouth opened wide. She could not believe what she was seeing. There, in front of her, was the most beautiful land she had ever seen. It was a land of candy and other delights. Fountains of sweet, pink lemonade, trees made of sugar cane and gum drops, flowers with petals of milk chocolate. Captain Mary tested the air, then took off her helmet (S.E.). She and Torbik ran to the pink lemonade fountains and began to drink (S.E.).

Then they ate some of every kind of sweet. Torbik suddenly stopped moving and eating. All he could do was make a quiet little yelp (S.E.). Captain Mary leaned over Torbik (S.E.) and discovered that her robot dog was rusting. She pulled from her pocket a small can of oil and began oiling Torbik's joints. Torbik finally began to move his squeaking joints (S.E.). Eventually, well-oiled, he could move freely again. After that, Torbik kept away from the lemonade.

Suddenly, Captain Mary heard a sound like somebody jumping up and down in wet tennis shoes (S.E.). The sound came closer and closer (S.E.). All at once a funny-looking creature with four arms, four legs, and a comical hat appeared. The creature put out its two right hands to Captain Mary. At first the Captain was frightened, but when she saw the big smile on the creature's face she decided it must be friendly. So she shook the creature's two right hands. It signaled to the Captain and Torbik to follow, so they did. Later they learned the creature's name was Zoobie Doobie Doo. Zoobie Doobie Doo gave them many more sweet things, and the Captain ate like a pig.

After "pigging out," Captain Mary sat down to rest. She was munching on a chocolate cookie when she suddenly felt a sharp pain in her tummy. "Ouch," she cried out as the pain hurt more and more. Tears rolled from her eyes. But Zoobie

Doobie Doo came to her rescue and gave her a strange ball that she was to shake. As the Captain shook the ball (S.E.), she could feel her eyes getting heavier. Finally, she dozed off to sleep.

The next thing Captain Mary saw was her bedroom with all her toys scattered about. As Mary jumped out of bed, she realized she had been dreaming. As she ran to the bathroom (S.E.) and began to brush her teeth (S.E.), she promised never to go to bed again without brushing her teeth, especially after eating sweets.

My Wonderful Balloon (A Sound Story)

The children plan for and present a creative dramatization of a sound story.

Activity

The children explore sound sources and experiment with ways to dramatize actions as they prepare for a creative dramatization of a sound story.

Procedure

Read the story to the children and help them become familiar with the sequence of events. (You may want to modify or abbreviate the story for the children in your group.) Ask them to suggest and try out ways to dramatize the various actions, and sounds to highlight certain events. The sound effects (S.E.) in the story are only suggestions; these may be omitted and others included. Also, names can be changed as children take turns role-playing the three characters.

Supplementary Activity

Invite the children to create another sound story about a bunch of different-colored balloons. Guide them to think of an original set of events for the story. Eventually write the story based on their suggestions, then rehearse it and later perform it for other children in the school.

Materials

Assorted rhythm instruments and sound sources for sound effects

My Wonderful Balloon (A Sound Story)

Cast: Sandra, Old Man, Balloon (child)

One windy and sunny day, little Sandra met a funny old man who said "Give me three pennies and I'll give you a wonderful balloon." Sandra reached into her pocket and brought out three pennies, which she gave to the old man. The old man gave Sandra a package with a balloon in it, then walked away. She was anxious to see the balloon and blow it up. She ripped open the package (S.E.) and a strange-looking balloon fell to the ground (child role-playing the balloon lying on the floor). Sandra saw it looked like a big toe. She found the end of the balloon and began to blow on it (lifts up a leg, cups her hands over the toe, and pantomimes blowing up the human balloon). She blew with all her might (S.E.). Slowly, the balloon filled with air, and as she blew harder and harder (S.E.) the balloon became bigger and bigger. Finally the balloon stood tall (human balloon standing), and Sandra was surprised to see her balloon was shaped like a little boy. But as she was holding on to her new, strange balloon, the wind began to blow very hard (S.E.), so hard it pulled the balloon away from her tight grip. Puttering and fluttering, the balloon spun round and round in a circle (S.E.) until all the air escaped, and it finally fell to the ground.

But Sandra did not give up. She started again to blow up her wonderful balloon. She blew and blew (S.E.) until the balloon finally filled with air once again (human balloon again standing). Sandra reached into her pocket for a piece of string to tie to the balloon's toe. Sandra was so happy! She ran and skipped all over town holding on to the string as her wonderful balloon followed her everywhere she went.

As Sandra joyfully went around town, a sudden, great wind started to blow. She held on tightly to the string. But the wind blew so hard (S.E.) it finally pulled the string from her hand, and the balloon floated away. Sandra raced after it. Each time she got closer to the string, the wind blew it away again. The wind blew Sandra's balloon over houses and trees (some children may role-play houses and trees), but she kept following and would not give up. Finally the balloon floated down on a beach and rocked gently back and forth in the sand (S.E.). "My, the sand is hot," thought Sandra as she gently tip-toed (S.E.) in the direction of her balloon. As she was ready to grab the string, another sudden wind gust (S.E.) blew the balloon away into the streets nearby. As Sandra chased the balloon, car and truck horns honked (S.E.), and the cars and trucks had to turn quickly to avoid hitting the balloon and Sandra. "Get out of the way," yelled one driver. Another shouted "Watch out, kid." When Sandra was safely out of the street she looked around but could no longer see her balloon.

Then, she looked up, and was surprised to find the string of her balloon stuck on telephone wires. Three big boys came by, and they too saw the balloon. They began to throw rocks at it. Sandra tried to stop them but they ignored her pleas. Then one of the boys threw a rock with all his might and Sandra's wonderful balloon went POP! As the pieces of the balloon came fluttering down, the boys walked away laughing (S.E.). Sandra, very sadly, picked up the pieces of her broken balloon. Suddenly, the old man appeared, tapped Sandra on the shoulder (S.E.), and gave her another package with a balloon inside. Her face lit up with joy. She thanked the old man and took the package home without opening it. She decided not to take a chance on the wind blowing away another wonderful balloon.

Appendices

Index of Content Areas

List of Recorded Selections Used in the Book

Equipment List

Cassette tape recorder with recording tape (a second tape recorder is optional)

Set of rhythm instruments

Phonograph

Set of resonator bells (individual bells that may be removed from carrying case)

Several drums of different sizes

Film projector (16mm recommended, 8mm useable)

Leader film for size of projector available

Screen or white wall for projection

Three to six hula hoops

Large rubber or plastic ball

Autoharp

Sample Letter to Parents

Date

Dear Parents:

Our school is currently participating in a program of activities specifically planned to help your child develop creative abilities in art, music, dance, and drama. Occasionally, your child may take home a product of his or her creative efforts, and may wish to demonstrate some aspect of a creative activity in which he or she has participated. We encourage you, as opportunities are available, to talk about what your child is learning—even ask your child to teach you some of the creative skills developed in this program.

Following is an activity adapted from the materials we are using that you might participate in with your child.

> Suspend a sheet with a heavy cord or other means in an area where space is available both in front and back of the sheet. Place a bright lamp (or slide projector or film projector without film) about twelve feet behind the sheet, and take turns going behind the sheet to create interesting shadow designs with your body (lamp and performer on one side, audience on the other side). You also might use various objects in the house along with your bodies to create a greater variety of shadow designs. Make every effort to stimulate your child's imagination and encourage original ideas.

Should you have any questions concerning this program of creative activities—or any other aspect of our school program—please call or visit the school. We will make every effort to help you gain a better understanding of our school's goals.

Cordially,

(name), Director

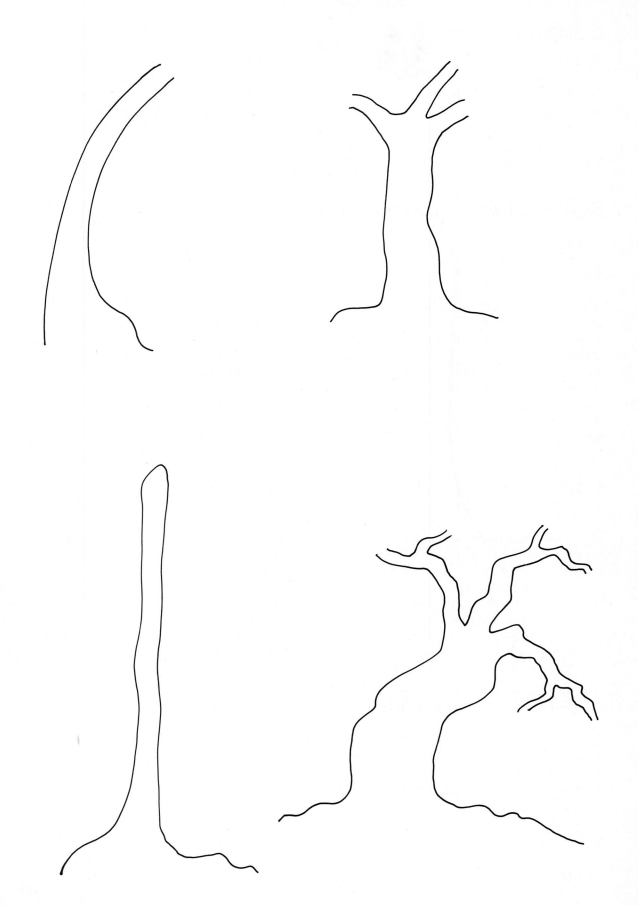

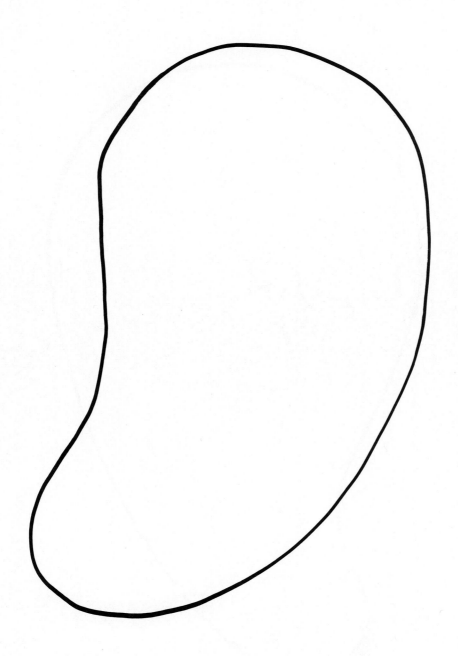

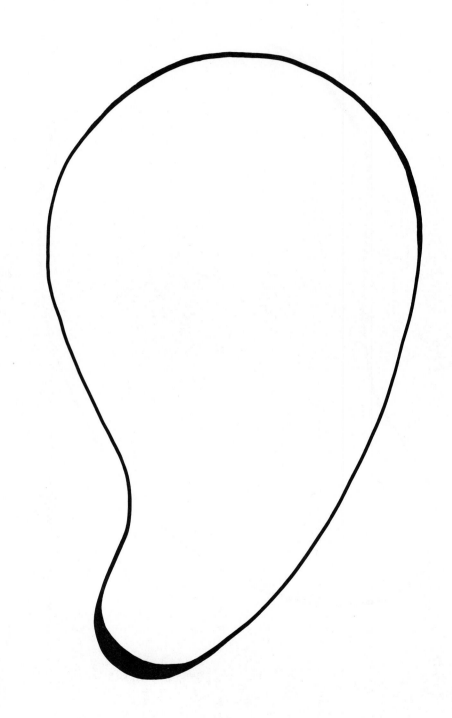

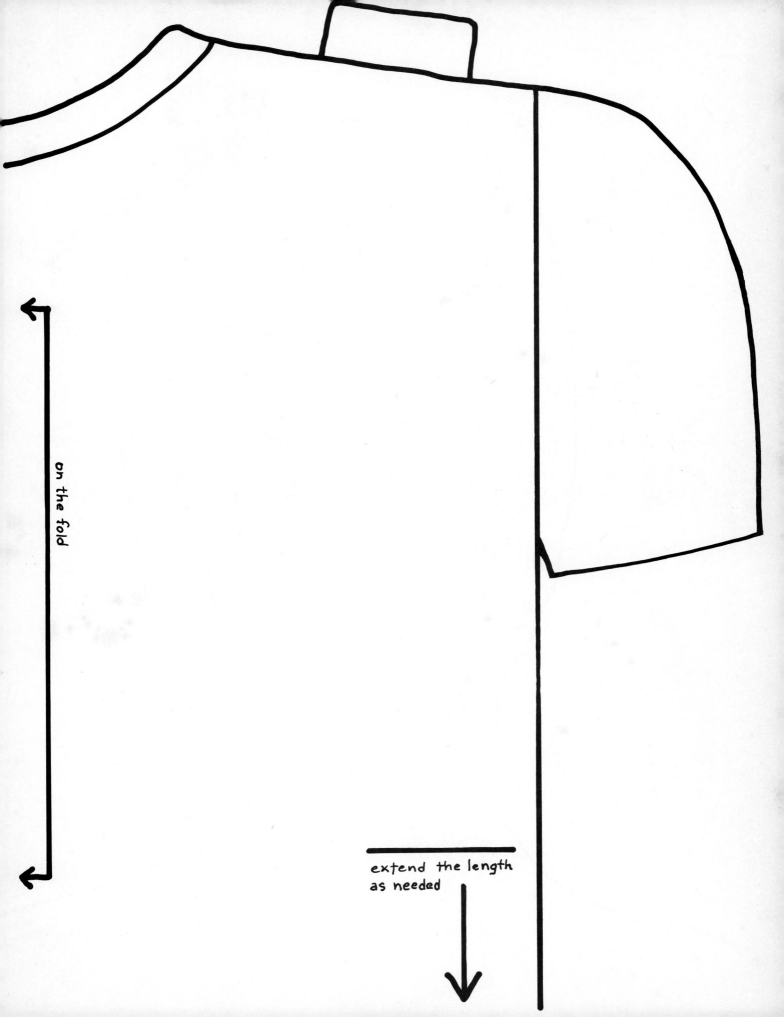

on the fold

extend the length
as needed

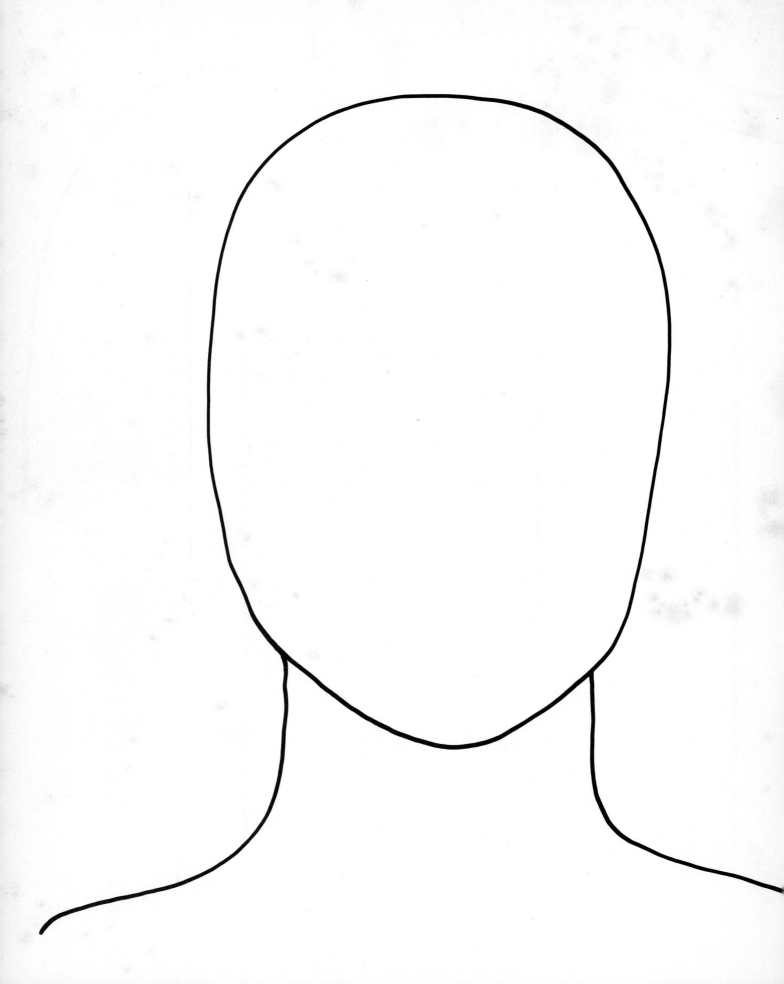